Praise for

FAILURE DISRUPTED

"Laying the groundwork for a successful start-up and organizational team requires a skilled leader, one who has the ability to solve problems and seize opportunities as they come. *Failure Disrupted* is clear, compelling, and shows founders, entrepreneurs, and CXOs exactly how to find their way."

JOSH LINKNER, five-time tech entrepreneur, *New York Times* bestselling author, and venture capitalist

"Choosing fulfillment as an entrepreneur or business leader requires that you create something of significance. Johnnie Garmon has given you the formula to not only create it, but also sustain it."

MARSHALL GOLDSMITH, #1 *New York Times* bestselling author of *The Earned Life* and *What Got You Here Won't Get You There*

"Johnnie Garmon's business-building experience has proven uniquely insightful and invaluable for any business founder, owner, or CEO. Inside are true insights into the undeniable impact any leader can have."

GINO WICKMAN, author of *Traction* and *Shine*, creator of EOS® (Entrepreneurial Operating System)

"Think you understand what it takes to run a successful business? This book will open your mind to new possibilities and increase your impact as an entrepreneur."

JONAH BERGER, bestselling author of *Contagious* and *The Catalyst*

"We only learn how to do hard things and accomplish big goals by getting advice from people who have done it before. That's the gift of Johnnie Garmon's personal, powerful story and the steps he used to take 'failure' and transform it to achieve great success. It's hard for any entrepreneur or business leader to put this book down because you want to be a part of the evolution and clear success strategies outlined herein. Grab your notepad and enjoy the ride!"

CAROLINE MILLER, MAPP; #1 Goals & Grit™ guru; eight-time bestselling author of *Big Goals, Creating Your Best Life,* and *Getting Grit,* among others

"In the cluttered world of business books designed to help entrepreneurs, Johnnie Garmon's *Failure Disrupted* stands heads above the rest. It is filled with practicality and clear organization, and outlines his success in an easy-to-read style. Johnnie speaks from a place of real-world business experience—not classroom theory."

DR. HANS FINZEL, leadership mentor and bestselling author of *The Top Ten Mistakes Leaders Make*

JOHNNIE GARMON

FAILURE DISRUPTED

Clear Milestones *for* Entrepreneur *and* Business Leader Success

www.amplifypublishinggroup.com

Failure Disrupted: Clear Milestones for Entrepreneur and Business Leader Success

For more information, please contact:
Amplify Publishing, an imprint of Amplify Publishing Group
620 Herndon Parkway, Suite 220
Herndon, VA 20170
info@amplifypublishing.com

Library of Congress Control Number: 2025909455

CPSIA Code: PRV0525A

ISBN-13: 979-8-89138-659-4

Printed in United States

This is for all of you who have the courage to step out and ask for a better day tomorrow.

WHERE ARE YOU IN YOUR JOURNEY?

WHERE DO YOU WANT TO BE?

It can be challenging to know these answers when you don't know what questions to ask.

Take the Milestone Map Test.

Find your answers.

Clarify where you need to go.

theperissosgroup.com

Contents

MAKE IT SUSTAINABLE

I HAVE BEEN THERE TOO!

I still remember that sunny day in mid-September 2010. My Hallmark Hospice colleagues and I had taken to the links at The Preserve at Verdae Golf Club in Greenville, South Carolina, to play in a fundraiser for local charities. It was just shy of the two-year anniversary of my accepting the role as Hallmark's executive director.

When I arrived, the company was a start-up with six months under their belt and over a half-million dollars in debt. They were facing two choices: get out of the red or shut down. After shotgunning resumes across the state to companies on the hospice registry, Hallmark had been among those who responded. It was clear that the company's pain points were not unlike those I had seen across other agencies. There was an opportunity for greater communication; they were suffering from excess turnover; and they were being weighed down by a lack of morale. With just over a year of healthcare experience behind me, I had enough arrogance and just enough ignorance to believe I had what it took to grow this startup.

Having made the transition into hospice the year before, I had fallen in love with the mission of the industry. From the day I began, the work beckoned me because I knew that I wanted to change lives. And I was excited about serving in a leadership role within an organization that had yet to find its identity. The company's COO loved how well I understood the issues they were facing and asked if I could give their turnaround a shot. It was clear he felt they really didn't have much to lose by gambling on a young, confident country boy with only a year of experience. The COO said, "We'll give you a shot, but if you don't turn it around in six months, we are closing it and you are out of a job."

And so, I took the leap!

For two years, I worked hard to prove myself, bridging the perspectives of the different parties within the agency and aligning them with a common goal. I didn't yet know all the nuances of the business, but I did understand the nuance of people. They were what makes the difference in any endeavor.

When the team at Hallmark rallied around and started acting upon the new foundational values, magic began to happen. The company went from swimming in a sea of debt to turning a profit over $3.5 million. Turnover had become nearly non-existent, their quality measures with Medicare were impeccable, and the bottom line was healthily increasing.

Yet as Hallmark's medical director and my trusted colleague, Romin, and I made our way down the first fairway at The Preserve, it felt as though the other members of the executive team were treating me differently. As we hit the second hole, there was no denying the building sense of uneasiness. It was coming from the corporate clique, and I never really made inroads with the good ol' boys club. I didn't necessarily play the game of the higher-ups; I had chosen to focus on our team and patients, rather than personalities and office politics. It all led to an old feeling of often having been boxed out—one that I had stuffed down deep within myself—but again was rising to the surface.

Midway through our game, as we headed down the fairway of a par five, Romin said to me, "Dude, something *is* different. I think they are about to fire you." There was no denying his words; I felt them too. The following Monday morning, I was called in to the corporate office and let go from a job I had moved across the state to pursue. Even though Romin and I had a feeling it was coming, when our COO delivered the news, it stung. I had never seen myself as the kind of person to be terminated, as I had always dedicated myself to being a hard worker. There also hadn't been a single moment over the two years that I hadn't treated the company, their team, or their budget as if it were my own.

Upon hearing the case that Hallmark's management had made for my termination, I was hardly granted an opportunity to share my perspective. Their reasons seemed to lack any rationale, outside of my knowing the company had reached a point where they could sell and may have begun making cuts in advance of doing so. Being a firm believer that facts are a mere annoyance to someone who has already made up their mind, I didn't fight back. I wasn't going to play the game. Scribbling my resignation letter on a scratch piece of paper, I pushed it across my boss's desk and suggested that we just all save ourselves the time and theatrics.

The company's HR Director drove me home and took back possession of my company car, leaving me standing at the doorstep of the two-story Easley, South Carolina, home I had just purchased. There I was, alone and questioning everything. I felt cheated and disrespected. The loss of my role was difficult to stomach, sending me into a spiral of expected questions. *How could they do this to me? How could they do so right before my quarterly bonus was due to be paid?* It felt as though politics had directed their decision, and I was left feeling like an outsider rejected by a town I had been working so hard to make my home. Another door had closed; it felt as though I had failed.

Having to walk away from Hallmark led me back to the unsettling uncertainty of standing at a familiar crossroads. Four years earlier, in the thick of my divorce, I had made the shift from being an operations manager in the construction field to unexpectedly moving into a human resource role in the hospice industry. During a time where I had felt unprepared to be a husband or a single father, I leapt, headfirst, into a role for which I was also completely unqualified. I did it because I wanted to get to know an industry that was truly helping people, and the idea of entering the hospice care field intrigued me. Starting work with Mercy Care, the first agency to hire me after I left the construction and development industry, had felt like the greatest possible contrast to complaints about hairline fractures on the ceilings of multi-million-dollar homes, barely identifiable misalignments of beams, or arguments over the color of the drapes that had become a part of every day in the world of new construction.

Working in hospice quickly showed me that patients wanted nothing more than a better day today than yesterday. They wanted to be able to define what that meant, on their own terms. Looking forward, after being fired from Hallmark, not only did I want a better day for myself today, I wanted an even better day tomorrow.

Hospice care was a small niche industry, and everyone seemed to know everyone. Within a matter of days, word had spread that I had become available; my phone began to ring with offers from those who knew the transformations I had helped conduct at both Mercy Care and Hallmark. It would have been easy to justify going back to work for someone else, but with every opportunity to interview with other companies, I found myself becoming increasingly discouraged. *How could I go work for others who knew and cared less about the business than I did? How could I be a part of something that looked at people in need of medical care solely as a means to a better bottom line?* I knew what the numbers were and what profit margins looked like. Was anyone else going to understand or believe what had become clear to me: that helping the patients was the true goal? I had my doubts. No longer did I want my future to lie in the hands of someone I couldn't trust, nor did I want to be pouring myself into building someone else's dream. I had to strike out on my own, knowing the impact of the work was what mattered most to me.

The frustrations and pain I endured were the price of admission to prepare me for the person I needed to become. Going through my journey as a father, husband, friend, and team leader had granted me perspective, even through the pain. Looking back, I could see paralleled waypoints to be navigated during the circumstances I perceived as failures. I could also see how there was power in shifting these moments in time, using them as stepping stones and catalysts for success. This cycle replaying itself over and over again in my life could either lead to frustration or growth from this point forward. As I would have wished for anyone else, I chose growth.

FAILURE DISRUPTED

TODAY, THINGS CHANGE

Failure! You have felt it before. You plant healthy seeds with the best of intentions, but you still get weeds. You don't have to go looking for it to find you. Chaos, entropy, and a default to failure are constantly lurking, attempting to form speedbumps on the pathway of your best intentions. No matter how hard you try to prevent it, failure can feel pervasive, always waiting to strike when you take your eyes off the target.

Today, things must change. No longer will you stand for the status quo. As a founder, entrepreneur, team leader, or head of your organization, you are ready to act in defiance of current systems and forecasted downfalls. Why? Because you know that when you do what others have done, or what you always did before, you will *not* get the same results … *you will get less*! This is because your environment has already changed—a new rule has come into place or a new competitor has entered your space. It's time to think differently, to grow as a leader, to work with intention, to disrupt failure, and to fuel success.

Before we get started, let me clarify one thing: failure is never final. Failure is not the end of the road. Most people perceive defeat as an unwanted result, rather than a stepping stone to a much greater *yes*. Failure serves as a starting point for a vision of shaping a better tomorrow for everyone. Sometimes it is the equivalent of hearing "*not yet,*" instead of the crippling "*no*" it is perceived to be. The truth is that failure is not possible when you are intentionally pursuing a vision. Even when you "fail" to create the outcome you initially set out to achieve, you will have grown along the way, so long as you are learning and adjusting your approach—doing things better than you did yesterday. There will never be failure in that.

If you are tired of living by the status quo and settling for standard, ill-fated circumstances and outcomes, welcome home. Anyone can get things right once, without having all the answers. However, it takes a clear roadmap of milestones, turning points, and landmarks to fulfill and sustain a vision, while growing into who you are intended to become as a leader. *Failure Disrupted* offers more than just a roadmap for success. It is a strategy and a call to arms for leaders and visionaries who are determined to disrupt outdated paradigms and are ready to lean into cultivating resilience. It provides proven principles that will allow you to shape a team or enterprise built to withstand the tests of time. It is a blueprint for becoming an active force for good and for growth. Follow the steps and adopt the proven tools, and you will create a culture of success, a way to navigate the inevitable challenges, and ultimately, turn your vision into a successful reality.

The map that is going to help you disrupt failure is what I call the Milestone Map:

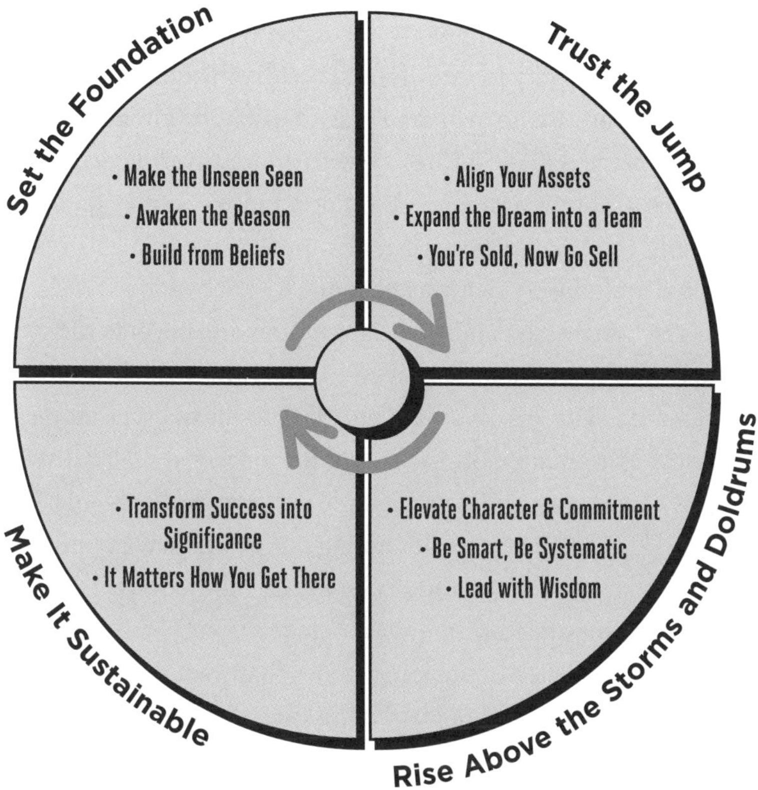

As the founder of Providence Care—the little faith-filled health-care startup I dove into after being fired from Hallmark, and which flourished against all odds—I wish I had had these steps and map before I started, instead of being forced to learn through trial and error. During my tenure, I learned so much about the distance that must be travelled and lessons that must be learned to reach a place of real success.

As I navigated the tumultuous waters of building a thriving healthcare startup, I discovered that the greatest lessons often emerge from setbacks. Each challenge I faced revealed a unique pattern of growth: even in moments of perceived failure, there was a marked opportunity for transformation. Truth be told, many days it felt like I was sewing my parachute after having already jumped out of the plane. I made it through with an unwavering dedication to a vision and by leaning on my values. I also chose to do things differently than the biggest players in healthcare and as a result, disrupted an industry that was past-due for innovation.

As the business expanded to eight-figures and beyond, the pain, triumphs, luck, and setbacks began to paint a picture of what success required. The answers were not clear to me in every moment, but a close examination of each step of the journey revealed distinct patterns. A sequential and predictable process emerged—one that is essential to the journey of disrupting failure and navigating decisions, transforming an initial vision into a fulfilled dream. What lay behind and ahead of me was a clear trajectory of repeated milestones, paralleled by stepping stones that were either being hit or missed. Studying and documenting everything along this journey, it became clear that this trajectory was playing out not only in my life, but also in the lives and enterprises of others.

Everyone thinks you have all the answers when you are the one with the vision. This is simply not true. For many years, I ran the business as if I were driving a car and relying on the rear-view mirror. I didn't know that I had hit a wall until I felt the crash. This book will save you from experiencing the same impact by helping you keep your eye on the road in front of you. It will guide your process of building a vision, your leadership ability, and a cohesive team. It is the manual for knowing where you are in the journey and anticipating what comes next, both of which are essential to success. Why? Because anticipation leads to preparation and preparation is power. Anticipation is also a close partner to the hacks required to navigate times that will test your character, commitment, and ability to sail through even the roughest seas. You will need it in order to reach the shores of impact and sustainability.

Your ability to grow lies in direct proportion to your ability to shoulder the weight. Things will get better and the vision you have for your team or organization will be fulfilled when *you* get better! Internal growth will always precede external growth. This repeatable cycle is designed to help you grow into the leader you need to become. This proven model has served as the basis for creating not just one, but five companies, all working together under one purpose. Welcome to a world where leadership development and business development run in parallel.

Success should never be a surprise, nor should failure. *Now* is the right season to pursue the outcome you want and to dedicate yourself completely to that ideal target. Choose to never be a victim of your circumstances and you will become a true victor within your achievements. Whether you are leading a team within a larger enterprise or starting from ground zero and founding your own, this manual offers a bold manifesto for those ready to challenge the status quo. It's not enough just to go through the motions and shape something. You must work hard to ensure your impact has longevity. It's time to stare failure defiantly in the face, redefining it as a stepping stone rather than a sinkhole.

Walk in a spirit of confidence.

Follow the trajectory you are destined to fulfill.

Act with intention.

This road map in *Failure Disrupted* is my gift to you. It will enable you to forecast the coming steps, as you progress from a vision to your reality. You will gain the understanding that failure is not a dead end, but rather the first step toward success. My goal is for you to walk away from this book feeling like you've got this—because I know you do!

Your journey toward impactful leadership and organizational growth starts here, as you take the steps to disrupt failure.

SET THE FOUNDATION

As a leader, you are not at the top of a pyramid.

You are the foundation—the base that holds up everything else.

MILESTONE 1: MAKE THE UNSEEN SEEN

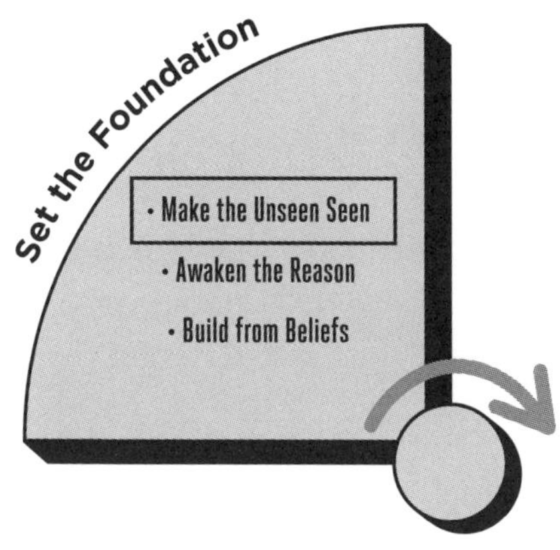

MAKE THE UNSEEN SEEN

Pastor Jeff Dunn at the Methodist church in Myrtle Beach, South Carolina, is someone I always felt to be an electric speaker. A tall, fit minister in his early forties, he always wore a non-traditional white, collared, long-sleeve shirt and jeans. Standing on the stage in the converted theatre space, his words had a powerful way of cutting through the room, resonating with all of the congregation.

While many of his sermons hit home with me, I will never forget the day he asked us to contemplate *foundations*. Engaging the room, he questioned what we would notice when driving up to a beautiful hotel, resort, or conference center. Walking inside, chances are we would take note of the enchanting front doors, the grand entrance, the striking bar, or the beautiful décor. Undoubtedly, selfies would be taken in front of the magnificent chandeliers or the floor-to-ceiling fireplace. Yet, how many of us would walk outside and admire the building's foundation? Who among us ever stops to appreciate a sturdy, well-built base? It's ironic, he told the room, because without it, the rest of the hotel or resort would not even be there . . . nor would it stand the test of time.

Pastor Dunn's words never left me; they became the base for how I went on to teach and build foundations. Disrupting failure starts with a solid foundation. Whether you are leading or founding—a team, an enterprise, a for-profit, or a nonprofit—the ultimate outcome of what you are building will always begin with a clear picture of where you are going ... but there is more to it than that. Your work must begin by laying a foundation for what will hold up your vision. You do it by being innovative regarding how you see opportunity and strategic about when the time (or season) is right to jump in.

You need to ensure the sustainability of your impact in order to fulfill your vision, and become all that you are intended to be. Clearly visualizing where you want to go and what you want to achieve are not enough on their own. You also need to be keenly aware of what will keep you moving toward your goals and what kind of culture you want to shape along the way. These are the first elements of a foundation and the basis of the first step of the Milestone Map: "Make the unseen seen."

Counter to the popular adage, a journey doesn't begin with a first step. It begins with an intention—a purpose statement, an outcome, a goal, an objective, a vision of what could be—and the belief that this destination is actually achievable. That foundation is about faith—not just believing, but *knowing* the check is in the mail long before it has arrived. It is about trusting that you will indeed build the team, company, or community you envision; and that you will grow in some way every day.

It's easy to want to jump in and immediately attempt to reach for the peak of your profession. However, doing so often means you may not dedicate the necessary attention to building the required solid foundation. Without contemplation and planning, reaching your destination and fulfilling your vision is either not going to happen, is going to end up misdirected, or will be not nearly as fulfilling as it ultimately could be. Love on your foundation, because when you get these pieces right, the rest is going to follow with even greater impact and longevity.

What Right Looks Like

Working for Mercy Care and Hallmark Hospice, I witnessed many people in the industry making things more difficult than they needed to be. I saw agencies create systems that forced patients to conform—to fit into boxes that needed to be checked. It was not a healthcare system that tailored to the individual needs of the patient. Too many seemed unwilling to be inconvenienced to support populations that remained underserved and in great need. That included those who lived in less-than-ideal areas or homes that lacked what was considered a standard of cleanliness, veterans living in hotel rooms, or illegal immigrants with no way to pay for the care they needed. Left uncared for, these people had only one access point to receiving support—through the back of an ambulance to the emergency room doors.

Since my final day at Hallmark, I had developed an unwavering desire to do something to disrupt the heavily regulated world of end-of-life care. I wanted to become a part of the solution by providing the underserved population with pre-acute care—the kind of healthcare that prevented acute care from ever becoming necessary. I was no longer willing to accept how things had been run under the *status quo.*

In September 2010, Providence Care began from the kitchen nook in my home. It was an end-of-life agency created to make the unseen seen and overserve the underserved. If the venture worked, it would indeed be providential—an act of God—given the obstacles we faced. The cost to launch would be at least half a million dollars. The first six to twelve months would be funded totally out-of-pocket, as we worked to get our Department of Health surveys and become licensed by the state, all the while proving our competence to qualify for Medicare and insurance reimbursements. I would need nurses, social workers, a doctor, and an administrator. It would also require some extremely creative math to make it all happen with the $25,000 I had sitting in my bank account.

Venturing out as an entrepreneur felt enticing. But the truth was that I felt totally unqualified to launch a company. The past few years of my work in hospice care had provided great lessons about the industry, but I still had so much to learn. I was not fearless; I had plenty of doubt. Yet if I was going to fail, I wanted it to be under my control.

Those in search of identifying counterfeit money don't study what fraudulent bills look like; they study legitimate bills. They know *what right looks like.* They make no effort and waste no time contemplating anything that is not the authentic product. If you are going to force yourself off a cliff into the unknown, you need to know exactly where you want to go and what right looks like for you. By defining what you believe to be right, and by having that vision become your unwavering destination, you create a focus that keeps you from getting lost. It lays the groundwork for a solid foundation, built to disrupt failure.

Making the unseen seen—by forming your vision of what right looks like—is about identifying opportunities and solutions where everyone else sees problems or blindly accepts the *status quo*. This is your first step to imagining a better tomorrow as you pursue something more, something different, something that fully aligns with who you want to become! Much like my personal quest to be the one to overserve the underserved, you must begin with the end in mind. This happens when you define your ultimate outcome—the goal line you are willing to fully dedicate yourself to reaching.

To create the full picture of what your vision is intended to be, look outside yourself. Your vision is never yours alone. It is not just about you! As we'll discuss later in the book, one thing I always like to say is it is *for* you, but it's not really for *you*. Meaning, even though you are the one spearheading the vision, it ultimately has to be about something bigger, such as the world you want to impact and serving those around you. As you define your external environment to become a parallel reflection of what you believe is possible, ask yourself:

- *Is there a current problem to be solved or opportunity to be seized?*
- *Does your vision make the world better? Does it offer more value than others are currently offering?*
- *How does your vision affect those around you? What is the overall cost to yourself and others? Does the realized destination outweigh the cost?*
- *If you are venturing into entrepreneurship, can your vision be fully monetized?*
- *Did you write out and conceptualize your goal?*

There is no limit to what your vision can entail; what matters is that you believe and trust in it unequivocally. The most powerful checkpoint for the validity of your vision for what right looks like is found within you. More than positive thinking, this is about positive knowing. You must believe in what you think is possible, with every ounce of your being. You can't lie to yourself, and your body knows when you truly believe or are walking in doubt. As you begin to piece together your ultimate vision, ask yourself:

- *Does the goal feel like it's part of the identity you want to become?*
- *Is this undeniably your passion?*
- *Is this something you would wake up and pursue every day for free?*

Your vision must be the driving passion that wakes you up every morning wanting to be, do, and feel—one that makes you better with every day that you pursue it. It is so much more than simply having a good idea, wishful thinking, or a haphazard interest. This is about seeing an opportunity to create more value than currently exists and contributing something that truly helps those around you. The goal of any vision always has to be to improve the quality of life for most people, without damaging others in the process.

This work encompasses all three levels of the creative process: you think, you speak, and then you act. What you envision creating begins as a thought (a vision), which will then become more solidified as you start talking about it; then as you begin taking action, it becomes increasingly real. The progression from a thought in your mind, to words from your mouth, to actions from your body will stretch and challenge you in ways you previously thought unimaginable. What matters most throughout the process of disrupting failure is that once you have your vision, do not allow it to change! Hold tightly to the clarity of what you believe right looks like; be unwilling to settle for what is not. Establishing this unshakeable belief up front will give you the clarity that is critical to deliver success. It will influence your behavior, from this point forward.

Look at the Spaces In Between

In whatever role you serve, your ability to move the needle and stand the test of time will often be based on your ability to see possibility where others have not. Many times, you can find your vision in the in-between spaces. When training my staff, I like to ask a powerful question: "When you are driving down a highway, and the stated maximum speed is fifty-five miles per hour and the minimum is forty-five, how fast can you go based on the law?"

The answers almost always are that fifty-five miles per hour is the fastest you can go, with forty-five miles per hour being the slowest. However, that is not true. I asked how fast they *could* go, not the fastest speed they could legally drive. The truth is you can drive anywhere between forty-five and fifty-five miles per hour. There is an entire range that most did not see. There is so much more possibility than has been identified! So don't just look at the extremes, focus on the in-betweens and the possibilities.

Making the unseen seen is about envisioning the invisible and making it obtainable. You were perfectly happy with your flip phone until someone showed you what could be with a smartphone! You hadn't realized that such a thing was even possible or how much you wanted it, until someone showed one to you. It's about creating something new as much as it is improving on what is already there. The ability to identify the unseen means looking outside the status quo, into the special spaces that most overlook.

- *Can you note what is possible in the in-between?*
- *Can you live and think between the extremes?*

Great leaders can and do! Choose to think in new ways. When you do, making your vision a possibility will become something that allows true innovation and disruption to take place.

The Right Thing at the Right Time (Seasons and Cycles)

Sir Edmund Hillary and his sherpa, Tenzing Norgay, didn't just stumble upon the summit of Mount Everest while out for a stroll on May 29, 1953.[1] They became the first to summit the world's highest mountain only thanks to having a clear purpose; plenty of planning; adequate preparation; and consideration of the team, its skills, and the seasons. Preparing with a solid vision and seizing the exact season is what got Hillary to the top of Everest.

Blind belief is not enough. As Ecclesiastes 3:1 says, "To everything there is a season, and a time to every purpose under heaven." Pay attention to this. Once you have your vision, it is critical to understand that everything has both cycles and seasons. You won't succeed constantly swimming against the tide. A farmer can't plant their crops in the dead of winter and expect a harvest, and you can't face east expecting to see a sunset no matter how much you believe you will. Belief must always be married with wisdom. Despite one's best efforts, no one is going to revive Blockbuster or any other video rental store simply because of their nostalgic vision to resurrect the past. The season for these opportunities has long passed.

Timing and directionality are everything. A clear picture of your vision is worthless when you are pointing in the right direction but are unable to move forward. You need to know when the right time is to do the right thing. That's why the immediate next step to having a vision of what right looks like is to question whether what you envision is *in* or *out of season.*

Here's an example many of us can relate to: consider being in the place (perhaps many years ago), where you were considering becoming a spouse or parent. Hopefully, you thought about the attributes of a good spouse or parent (what right looks like). The next step would involve asking yourself if you are in season—i.e., whether you can currently give the relationship all that it requires. Knowing when your vision is in season is crucial to making the unseen seen for the team and people you are serving.

When you are a business owner or managing a corporate team, being in season has everything to do with your chances for success.* Knowing when you are in season boils down to knowing if you have enough resources, passion, and ability to support your vision. Do the right thing at the right time and you will be able to lean into natural rhythms to propel your vision forward. You won't be planting in winter or swimming out

* Success is what I define as anything that supports moving things forward in the pursuit of a goal, without hurting other people. It is an intentional daily pursuit and an alignment of things being in season.

against an incoming tide. Doing the right thing at the wrong time will only lead to pain.

The right thing at the right time means finding your ideal entry point in the cycle. There will be times when you have to simply pause and be patient, as you wait for your season to arrive. The timing is never going to be perfect, but when most of the arrows are pointing to things being in season, it's time to jump in. Just remember to move toward success, not perfection. Pause and see the possibility that lies in the in-between, but don't waste time looking for one-hundred percent certainty; as soon as you think you have it, something will have already changed! An eighty percent chance of success may be more than good enough in most cases—with the exception of gauging whether to fly on a plane. Some things require absolute certainty in order to progress, but many do not. Be mindful of your tolerance for risk and the requirements of the arena in which you find yourself.

The Key Questions

To get the right answers, you must ask the right questions. The quality of your life will always be in direct proportion to the questions you ask and the wisdom with which you make use of the answers. Even great leaders seldom have the right answers, but they almost always have the right questions! Questions drive everything we do. They hold the power to break things down to their simplest form, making things faster, more accurate, and easier to manage. They elicit clarity, and clarity is power. As you read each chapter, carry these *key questions* with you—on paper, in your mind and in your heart. These are the guideposts that will help move you forward, as you progress to fully disrupt failure.

Make the Unseen Seen

- What Right Looks Like:
    - *How are you going to create more value than anyone else?*
    - *Who do you need to become in order to achieve this?*
    - *Imagine you are eighty years old and have pursued your vision for all the years of your life. Is this the legacy you want? Does the execution align with and support who you want to become?*
- Look at the Spaces In Between:
    - *What is missing? What is the possibility that most are not seeing?*
    - *Are you seeing all that could exist, or do you need to step back and look again with new eyes?*
- The Right Thing at the Right Time:
    - *Are you doing the right thing at the right time by leaning into natural rhythms?*
    - *Or do you need to extend patience knowing what you envision is the right action, but it is just the wrong time?*

Take Action

---

1. **Reverse-engineer your destination:** From the end to the beginning, break down your vision from then to now. Even when you can't see what's coming, there is power in having an unshakable knowing in what you envision.
2. **Seek out new perspective:** Whether it involves stepping back and seeing things anew, or having others contribute new perspective, seek to see things differently than most people. Study the spaces in between for opportunity. Seek what many others may not think to find!
3. **Write down the reasons:** Why is it the right time for what you envision (the pros)? Why is it not (the cons)? Which list contains more? Look for trends and cycles. Nothing is static. Balance patience and effort, as you wait for your season to line up with your executional strengths. Then, when things are leaning most heavily toward the pros, it's time to dive in!

You may crave predictability, but when you are starting out in a new role, you have no choice but to lean into possibility. This stretching will involve a good dose of faith, and sometimes some dumb luck, because none of us can expect to be shown the full scope of what lies ahead. The pain or problem you want to alleviate may be clear as you formulate your vision, though *how* it is going to happen has not yet come fully into view. No matter how hard you try, you are never going to anticipate all of the twists and turns from the vantage point of starting out. Just know that and accept it. The plans you have, or what you think will work, may not. But things you have never considered as supports will show up. This is how providence works.

On the journey from here to there, having a clear vision of what right looks like, studying the spaces in between, and testing your seasons will mean that the foundation upon which you are building will be solid enough to hold the weight of what is yet to come. When the vision in your mind and the feeling in your heart are in sync, your belief in what is possible will turn into *knowing*. And when you know, you can move forward because the outcome feels secure. This conviction will draw others into your vision and be the catalyst for every step of the Milestone Map that follows, as you build or manage from the foundation up. Then, from here on, you are free to trust and have faith, knowing that your heart is clean, your intentions are pure, and you will continue to do the next right thing.

Motivation is the force that pushes you to continue beyond what is normal or expected, cutting through the distractions and rising to a higher set of standards.

MILESTONE 2: AWAKEN THE REASON

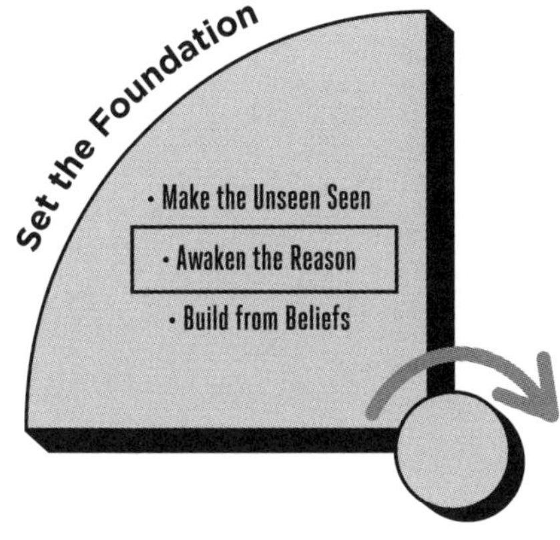

AWAKEN THE REASON

New Year's resolutions often come with the best of intentions. Christmas gifts of new workout gear or a gym membership bring forth hopes that this is the year of change. As the first of January rolls around, motivation levels are at an all-time high; there is a sense that exercising and better eating habits will stick. Hitting the pavement for a five-mile run on day one creates a feeling that this will indeed be the year the weight comes off and stamina returns. Then, the next run feels more challenging, as muscles remain tight and sore from the first attempt. Motivation feels harder to maintain, and the will to keep going requires a lot more. The third and fourth runs feel even harder. Truthfully, they almost didn't happen. Getting out of bed was a challenge in itself, given the strain on every muscle and an aching back. Before long, the motivation to get up every morning, and push to put in the miles, begins to falter. The initial excitement is all but lost.

Overly ambitious or unrealistic goals, a lack of a clear plan, and the inability to stay motivated when things get tough can stop you in your tracks. Why? Because they lead to the inability to improve on what you did yesterday—and that sets the stage for failure. Success requires clarity of our motivations and realism in our approach. Part of the reason for this runner's downfall was because their expectations were too high to begin with. In short, they overshot, and you can't build upon that. Instead of building up to longer runs and factoring in the required rest days needed to recover, they dove right in with five-mile runs. Their intentions may have been noble, but without taking incremental steps and factoring in how they were personally motivated, it became impossible to get where they wanted to go. They were set up for failure.

Take the small, monotonous, or boring steps consistently and build from there. The key to success lies in breaking down goals into manageable steps, staying focused on the motivating *why* behind your actions, and being consistent, even when the initial enthusiasm fades.

Every one of us has different motivations for accomplishing any worthwhile goal. Some strive for stardom, others for the thrill of the challenge. Finding your motivation—what is guiding you—is the second Milestone. It's about figuring out what's important to you. Why are you going to attempt to fulfill your vision? What is motivating you to pursue this grand idea? Is the realization of your vision worth the price you will pay? What can you lean on to keep you moving forward when things get hard? You had better know your *why*! An unwavering dedication to your vision happens when there is a deeper underlying motivation for why you are doing what you are doing.

You started this pursuit of what right looks like because you have chosen to raise your standards—you wanted something more for yourself, for others, for those you care about. As you embark on the journey of fulfilling your vision, you will inevitably reach points where you feel you have lost the will to push forward. When you only have a passive interest in what you are pursuing, then you will work toward it only when you *feel* like it. Such an inconsistent state can quickly become unreliable and destructive to your vision, especially when you fall deep into the doldrums. However, when you are *committed to* something, things change. As I like to say about motivation: you will lose it, so you must love your vision. Avoiding pain or seeking reward may have served as initial instigators; but only a passion will allow you to sustain your execution, especially because things *will* get hard.

The vision you have was never intended to simply be something you are passively interested in; it must be something you are committed to every day. This is about finding the actionable intersection of both internal and external factors that will continue to move you and the culture you are building forward. Then, when you reach a point where you feel you have run out of willpower, your commitment will become the fuel you can fall back on. It's the internal well of energy that helps you keep pushing ahead when things start to get hard, you are tired, you start looking for the off-ramps, or the novelty has worn off.

Your motivation must always be personal in order to truly move you. It comes from looking inside your mind and examining your heart, to understand the reasons why you are doing what you are doing. What is it that consumes the thoughts in your head? Whatever that burning desire is inside of you, it is your job to identify it and use it as the fuel for your journey. When you identify your motivation and attach it to your vision, then what you see as possible becomes exponentially more vivid, no matter how opaque or idealistic your goal.

Raise Your Standards, Raise the Stakes

Before knowing how I was going to create everything I envisioned for Providence Care, it was clear that I wanted to ignite a bigger vision—something that would create massive value for others. I was ready to stand for something better. Growing up on welfare and wearing hand-me-downs from my three older sisters sparked a certain discomfort early in life. For the four years leading up to the creation of Providence Care, I had worked to become a better leader and father. I wanted to better the hand I had been playing with and build the consistency and security that my daughter and I needed. This spurred me to visualize the possibility of what we could become. The vision fueled me with the determination to pursue it. I was motivated to become the best version of myself even before I understood what that meant. It felt as though the motivation behind my vision was clear—to create a better life for me and my daughter—and then it evolved into more than I could have ever anticipated.

A turn of fate brought my closest childhood friend, Kelley, to South Carolina. The moment we reconnected, we found in each other the friend we each truly needed at that point in our lives. With no intention of jumping into a romance, we found ourselves falling in love. As we began shaping a life together, a short engagement was made, and with marriage Kelley and her four-year-old daughter, Caroline, combined homes and families with me and my seven-year-old daughter, Reagan. As we all found ourselves blending together, things once again began to fall apart. I was fired from Hallmark.

Nothing about my becoming an entrepreneur made sense on paper, yet Kelley believed in me. She never questioned my vision. After helping me come up with the company name and foster the intention behind the agency, it became increasingly clear that she was willing to sacrifice her own desires for me to pursue what I believed in. I didn't know what the price would be to shape Providence Care, but I was willing to sacrifice for it, because there were now three people dependent upon me and my ability. I was determined to become better and turn my vision into a reality in order to create a better life for her and our girls. Every step I took became intentional, and every thought was resolute. I needed to win for them. If I couldn't get in through the front door, I would find a way through the back, and if that didn't work, windows would be my entry point. I would find a way.

When you are in the pursuit of excellence by creating value for those you serve, you have no choice but to raise your standards and inspire the same leveling-up for everyone else around you. Life is about increasing our standards—to do better, be better, create better—for ourselves and the people around us, with a vision for a better quality of life. You may desire an end result, but you need to have passion to inspire others to move the mountain with you. Your standards are literally the expression of what you stand for. They are what is authentic and real about you, guiding you to also clearly identify what is not. They are the first component of your motivation.

What are you determined to make better? What are you not going to allow yourself to ignore? We have to intentionally determine what our standards are, since most of us don't organically know them. Here's how you can do this:

- Write out a list of your current standards, and a list of the standards you are lacking. Compare the two lists. Where are the gaps you need to bridge?
- Consider those you are serving in your role. *How can they help you define your standards? What do you want for them? What current state do you see as unacceptable?*
- Look to people who are examples of what you want to be like. Take them to dinner or for a drink and pick their brain about what can be made possible.
- Talk to the elderly who have amassed a wealth of wisdom about life and the standards they did or didn't have. Allow those conversations to spark awareness of what standards resonate for you.

Nobody rises to low expectations. Without a constant focus to raise your standards, you will lower the standards of everyone around you, thereby not creating drive or momentum for those you need to continue to step up. When you don't have pronounced and defining standards, it will override your ability to be a good leader. It will feed failure, rather than success. Even when you don't know yet what your standards are and what right looks like, the pain you have experienced in your life can help define what your standards are *not*. Those experiences may show you that you want to ask for more in a relationship, how you want to become better at guiding a team, or define more clearly the next level of greatness you see as possible for your community or organization. Once you know what your standards are, there will no longer be room for what you feel is not right.

Heaven or Hell, Carrot or Stick

When I was operations manager at my brother-in-law's construction company, a young foreman named Josh told me he wanted to become a site manager. He had a lot of potential, but there were remaining tasks to be trialed in his current role—to show me that he could hold the responsibility of a leadership position. As I opened the door for him to prove himself, Josh continued to show up late, depart early, and leave tasks incomplete. Because I was personally motivated by rewards, I attempted to evoke a change in behavior by reiterating the potential for a raise and his taking the lead on some of the new builds we had forthcoming. Josh told me he'd do better and went back to work. Two weeks later, he was back in my office as we addressed the same complaints from customers: his tardiness and tasks left incomplete. Again, I tried to motivate him with all the possibilities he could achieve by addressing these weaknesses. The result was him nodding his head in agreement and returning to his same bad habits.

By our third conversation, I was done trying. My frustrations got the best of me, and I told him that if he didn't get his act in gear, I was going to take away his company truck, revoke his responsibility, and perhaps even demote or fire him. Out of frustration, I had unknowingly stumbled upon speaking his motivating language. To my surprise, Josh stood up from the chair at my desk and extended his hand to shake mine. In a moment where I felt as though I had been more threatening to him than I wanted to be, he thanked me for caring about him. He finally felt like I truly understood and heard him. Understood him? I felt like I was ready to throw him out of my office, and here he was, telling me he felt a connection and was suddenly motivated. After he left my office, I stared at the ceiling wondering what had just happened.

In no time at all, a light switch had been turned on, and Josh began doing everything he needed to do to achieve the next-level role. It became clear that his motivation was not the allure of pleasure, but the need to avoid pain. All I needed to do to help him move forward was show him what he was going to lose; because when you are motivated to move away from pain, no explanation of how great things are going to be will help move you forward.

As I grow older, I find my mind doing its best to create black-and-white scenarios from the grey areas of life. We don't live in a world of many true absolutes; but when you understand underlying motivations in yourself and others, you can lead and grow with greater clarity and intentionality. Based on all that I have experienced and witnessed, I still believe in the centuries-old two directives of motivation: toward the pursuit of pleasure or away from the discomfort of pain. It is important that you always recognize—both in yourself and in others—how you are primarily motivated. Your preference for one motivation over another will become your natural bias that influences your every move. You must be clear on what motivates you and those you work with, keeping this awareness top of mind in every interaction you take. Understanding this foundational aspect of motivation will help ensure that you not only remain encouraged to keep growing and progressing, but that you are also able to motivate the team that you build to support your vision. To understand whether you are moving away from pain or toward pleasure, ask yourself:

- *When you examine your vision, what do you see yourself moving away from? Is there a past pain you don't want to repeat?*
- *What do you see yourself gravitating toward? What is that "something better" that entices you?*
- *Is what you are moving toward bigger than what you are moving away from? Which of these two (pain or pleasure) is assuming the most prominent role in moving you?*

The fear of loss and the promise of gain will vary in how they influence your moving forward. Your motivation can change in relation to the size of the pain you want to move away from or gain you are drawn toward. One note of caution: don't make the mistake I initially made with Josh and step into the ring with the false belief that all motivations are the same as yours. Learn to understand what drives others and speak their language first. This will help you not only effectively lead and motivate others, but just as importantly, will help you lead yourself toward success.

Prepare, Create, and Celebrate

None of us, no matter how strong or heroic, can instantly jump from crawling to running a marathon. A fashion designer doesn't begin a business expecting their entire line to immediately take over the runways of New York Fashion Week, yet they may rejoice when their first design garners a positive online review or starts to trend. How do you keep motivated on what can seem like an endless journey to fulfilling your vision? You don't need to jump from zero to one hundred to bridge the gap between where you are to where you want to be; you can start by taking the step from zero to one.

Small wins are still forward progress. This is the only way to grow if you wish to sustain anything in life. Watch any NFL Sunday game; you will see a team come together and gleefully taunt the opposition over the few inches that earned them a critical first down. Counter this with an imaginary league where teams only celebrated if they won the game. It would make for far less exciting events and mean that only half of the teams would ever be celebrating. The rest would be left with nothing more than a loss and lacking motivation to foster their forward progress.

When a toddler takes their first few steps, parents rejoice, and there is resounding applause and encouragement for having accomplished a small, yet significant feat. The next day, that same toddler may take a few more steps, eliciting the celebration all over again. Small steps lead to big gains over time. As you travel the road to fulfilling your vision in a way that defies failure, challenge is inevitably going to find you and destabilize your mission. When it does, you need to refocus on what you can control in that moment. Regain momentum by reminding yourself of the love that is motivating you and by celebrating short-term wins. Like a child learning to walk, you have one big goal, but you also have to stop and cheer the smaller wins along the way. When celebrated, small feats will help remind you why you are willing to tread through the storms and doldrums—not to mention, the unknown. This action can make or break your motivation and your ability to keep moving forward.

Remembering to rejoice in small victories can be challenging in a society that defines countless celebrations as annual events—birthdays, Mother's Day, Father's Day, and whatever seasons you celebrate. I challenge you to think counter to the norm. How much longer will it take you to grow your vision into a reality if you are waiting on annual celebrations? The key to staying motivated is to continuously prepare, create, and celebrate *daily* as you progress. This means you are constantly striving for never-ending improvement as you prepare for each and every day, create new standards for yourself, and celebrate when a standard is achieved.

You will never be able to give what you don't have. In order to grow into a leader, one who motivates others to be what they are intended to be, you have to learn to find motivation within yourself first. In order to ensure you are always preparing, creating, and celebrating, ask yourself:

- *What small victories have you overlooked?*
- *What small successes will keep you moving forward when you are ready to quit?*
- *Are you one step closer to your goal today than yesterday?*
- *How can you approach things with new eyes, starting today?*
- *How can you begin to raise your standards?*

If you are waiting for big touchdowns or triumphs to celebrate, then you will eventually run out of momentum and your motivation will suffer. If you want to live a life of celebration, do it daily. Don't get too high on the highs or too low on the lows; nothing is forever. Life is not static. Regardless of what one day brings, get up and do it all again the next day, knowing that when you seek for something to celebrate, you will always find it. Such celebration will fuel the momentum you need to keep moving forward. Celebrating and raising standards on a regular basis will keep the flame of motivation burning. Keep doing so, even when you have moved ahead by only an inch, or are moving ahead in some areas but falling behind in others. Constantly remind yourself of why you are doing what you are doing. Hardwire it into your life, your business, your team, your relationships, and your family.

The Key Questions

Awaken the Reason

- Raise Your Standards, Raise the Stakes:
    - *What will be the bigger impact of your vision on those you love? On a larger population?*
    - *What current standards are unacceptably low to you? How would you elevate them?*
    - *What is your role giving yourself the opportunity to learn and become? How will this benefit those you are doing it for?*
- Heaven or Hell, Carrot or Stick:
    - *Who are the people you are attempting to help? What is pushing or pulling you to do so? (That is, are you driven by pleasure or pain?)*
    - *What are you willing to sacrifice to make your vision happen? What will help fuel this intent?*

- Prepare, Create, and Celebrate:
    - *Going forward, what can you dedicate yourself to celebrating every day?*
    - *Who are the people that celebrate alongside you, holding you accountable to fulfilling your vision of providing value for others?*

Take Action

---

1. **Keep elevating:** Always ask what the next level to your standards can be. Observe those you are supporting. Can you see them rising to the standards you have set? Or do they require further inspiration, such as even higher standards?
2. **Remember the pain of doing nothing:** Imagine the alternative of what things would look like without your execution. The pain of doing nothing will serve to keep you motivated. Allow this to empower you to break through barriers and fuel your passion for what you are doing. Remain open to the detours. Remember that while success can be celebrated by fixing a problem. Exceptional leaders can also celebrate the problem that was avoided to begin with.
3. **Constantly return to your vision and your *why*:** Remind yourself often of what you want to realize and

become, and why you are doing it. Can you feel the love you have for what you are doing and those for whom you are doing it? If you are more visual by nature, you can create a vision board for what you believe can be made possible and the motivation behind it.

4. **With every step forward, check in with your heart:** Let your inside be your compass. Checking in regularly with yourself will help you make sure everything you choose to do conforms with who you see yourself becoming. It will provide a gut check of whether or not you remain aligned with, and driven by, your identified motivation.

Without passion, there can be no sustainable profits. Many people skip the step of clearly identifying their motivating factors, feeling as though they can dive into the pragmatic details of a vision without stepping back and giving due consideration to the bigger picture. That is a mistake. In whatever role you assume, whether team leader, CEO, manager, or founder, motivation will permeate your entire journey to success. It ebbs and flows; it is not a constant. That is why you have to always be working to remind yourself *why* you are doing what you are doing. Your motivation should be ingrained in every fiber of your being and every moment of your day. Without taking the time to identify your motivating factors and remember why you started, the journey may become far too daunting for you to finish.

Clear motivation makes things grow to become more tangible, more personal, even in the moments when you feel you may be going in blind. Keen awareness of who you are and what is driving you will allow you to pause and reset when challenges arise. It will empower you to recommit to your vision when a challenge threatens to thrust you off course. Seek to always identify and understand your primary motivating factor (heaven or hell / pleasure or pain) and always celebrate the moments of small victory. This will allow you to keep working and not quit. Trust me when I say this work will become the fuel that serves you well into the future. Intertwine it with who you are and what you stand for, and you will be equipped for the long-haul.

Your culture is not a part of your business;
it *is* the business.

MILESTONE 3: BUILD FROM BELIEFS

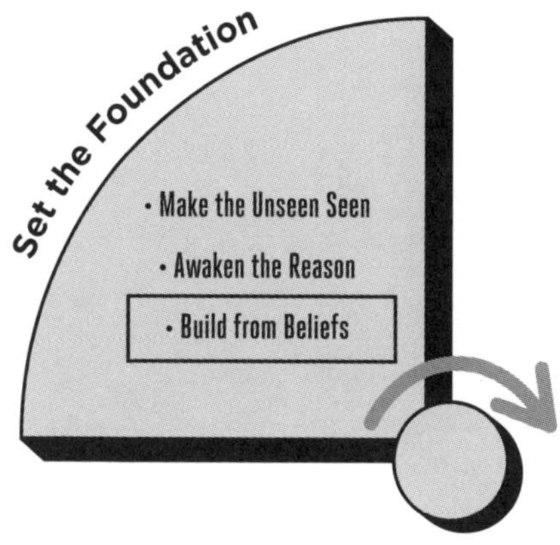

BUILD FROM BELIEFS

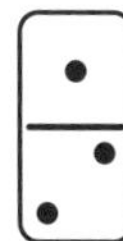

I hate mission statements. There, I said it. Despite being found in employee manuals, posted on office walls, and printed on letterhead shared with customers or vendors, how many employees can recite their company's mission statements verbatim? More importantly, how many are truly inspired by them?

While the intended purpose of mission statements is beneficial, they are often ineffective in their ability to inspire, motivate, and keep a team on course. Why? Because most mission statements lack emotional connection to the people involved and their beliefs—the true foundation of a culture. They are also often filled with technical jargon, sounding more like a college professor on a diatribe than a call to action proclaimed with a rebel yell!

In its simplest form, I define culture as "the way things are done around here." It is the action birthed from norms, rules, and traditions—both spoken and unspoken. It exhibits the core values, beliefs, or morals that are the underpinning of how people treat each other, along with processes and protections that are meant to be followed. Building on a foundation of your beliefs will have a lasting impact on your culture, as it affects how you think, how you speak, and ultimately how you act. Whether you are founding a company, guiding a team, or heading an enterprise or nonprofit, you are going to have a culture. And *when you don't choose it, it will choose you.* Leave culture to chance and it won't likely become what you want for yourself, those you are working with, or those you serve.

Have you ever listened to an orchestra tuning their instruments and practicing before a performance? It often sounds like a sea of uncoordinated noise. Everyone is playing different parts of the production and focusing solely on their own instrument. Then the show begins, and suddenly, everyone is playing from the same song sheet. The sound is incredible. These two polarities represent the difference between how things will go when you leave the formation of your culture to chance (or some ad hoc mission statement) and how things will look, sound, and feel when you build your culture from your beliefs.

You don't want to open the door to misalignment. When you are building a business or leading a team, your culture is not simply a part of your business; it *is* your business. As a leader, it is your responsibility to have a vision—what you want your team to achieve. It is up to you to facilitate the conversation by defining the values, beliefs, and language that will inspire you and those who are alongside you, to fulfill your vision. Because when those you are leading are out of tune with each other, things are going to sound, look, and feel like a mess of misaligned instruments.

There is a difference between founding a culture on beliefs versus an ad hoc mission statement. A clear outline of beliefs is remembered. It inspires. Most importantly, it dictates actions and can become adopted into the lexicon of everyone involved in the mission. This is the final step—and the third milestone—to setting a solid foundation upon which to build your vision and ensure that failure is disrupted.

Align Vision to Values

In my roles in the construction field and my early days working in hospice care, foundational work wasn't emphasized or even sometimes recognized. There were no core values at my brother-in-law's company, where I had acted as operations manager. When I arrived at Mercy Care, everyone seemed to be independently doing their own thing. (All I saw was a mess of misaligned instruments.) I could feel the lack of communication and pure chaos rippling through siloed departments. It was leading some of our best people to leave the agency, and our patients were the ones left suffering the greatest blow.

In an effort to bring everyone together under a common goal, I asked our best staff members what made them tick and started to recognize motivating factors that were spurring doctors, nurses, chaplains, and social workers to do life-changing work. I wanted to shine a spotlight on what was going well and create a guide for how (and who) we'd hire going forward. Following my year of experience at Mercy, having to help rebuild Hallmark taught me the importance of establishing core values or beliefs up front. I found myself putting even more emphasis than before on establishing them from the jump.

Somewhere between my roles at Mercy and Hallmark, I learned that people's beliefs were dictating what they were doing or not doing. They were the guiding force dictating whether each agency would be built to stand the test of time. When I decided to start Providence Care, it was clear to me: shaping the core values of a culture up front was crucial. *Culture must always precede growth.* It would have been easy to get bogged down on how I was going to turn my vision for Providence Care into a reality. It would have been simple to follow the expected pattern of going out and pounding the pavement to immediately drum up sales. But I knew it was foundational to make the message clear about the patient-centric focus behind our work. Without the strength of such a cultural underpinning, any growth would not endure. We would not truly be working together as a cohesive team.

On a small poster hanging in my line of sight, and on the desktop background that scrolled repeatedly on my computer, were five simple beliefs, fused with emotion. They were the core values I had shaped through my time at Mercy Care and Hallmark, and those I knew could carry Providence into the future:

- *We either add value or we don't do it*: "Does it add value?" was to serve as a qualifying question for every decision we make, from the front lines of patient care to bigger corporate spending decisions. Importantly, this value would never be equated to making money or not doing something in order to save money.
- *It's not about me, it's about we*: Having seen the power in team members helping each other and voluntarily putting in extra time, I knew the value of a collective mentality at the foundation of our work.

- *Consistent and limitless improvement*: As I grew older and technology grew quicker, like many, I witnessed innovation at a faster rate than ever before. It was evoking a requirement that we too continue improving, in order to keep pace and remain relevant. The rules of engagement are always changing, and trying to solve a problem that no longer exists is the reason many businesses failed. Improvement is centered around asking what problems need to be solved *today*.
- *We are where they are*: This point felt unique to hospice care, but it is potentially universal. More than simply meeting our patients where they were geographically, this was about levelling out with and understanding where they were spiritually, mentally, and emotionally, and doing everything we could to meet them there.
- *Everything happens for a reason, and it serves us*: To me, this value spoke to an ability to reframe and give empowering meaning to difficult circumstances. It was about taking a roadblock, a doldrum, or detour and choosing to learn from it, using it as a platform for growth. It was the same thing I had chosen to do after being terminated from Hallmark.

The quality of your culture will always be based on the quality of your own beliefs—your core values. They are the personal desires that motivate and guide your behavior. They are the things you are willing to live and die for, such as your relationship, service, integrity, and intimacy. Where your motivation becomes the driver to the fulfillment of the vision you have, your values give you direction and shape the team that will come together to make your vision a reality. When your motivation is in alignment with your values, you supercharge the potential fulfillment of your vision.

To grow a culture, each vision—like a distinctive personality—requires its own individualized declaration of beliefs. This means making a short list that clearly states what you want your team, organization, community, or family to be about. It should outline the core values and principles you hold dear and the standards to which you will hold yourself and all those who team up with you accountable. Defining the values at the foundation of your culture will serve to help you navigate the waters of tough decisions to come and will help you constantly evaluate if you are growing into who you intend to become. For everyone to steer their passion and skills in the direction you want things to go and sustain long-term momentum, you need to be clear on what core values define you. Continuously check in—with yourself and by observing the actions of others:

- *What touches your heart and evokes positive emotion for you?* The more inspiration you feel, the more aligned you are with your values and the more forward progress you will make. Our actions are always the most tangible representation of who we are as a person.
- *Does what you have just experienced feel right to you? Is it true to your nature? Do you feel that what you just did could have been done even better?* Gut-check what feels right. This doesn't always mean pinpointing wrong versus right; it's an opportunity to open up a

next level and further align with your deepest, most motivating beliefs.

- Study the stories of others. You can identify what you do and don't value when you see others acting in a certain way. *Are you inspired by their behavior or are you repelled by it? Can you see your values within their stories? What is the antithesis of the values that repelled you?* Knowing what you don't want is progress toward knowing what you do want.

Any of us can dream either in black and white or in color. The question is: how big a force for good do you want to become? Identifying and constantly revisiting your values will mean that you gain greater confidence and trust in your ability to execute your vision. When you value something, you are that much more likely to pursue it. The same goes for everyone you bring on board.

You don't need to know all your values to begin. Start by building awareness of your first two or three, and know that what you value will change and evolve over time. New experiences and personal evolutions will serve to both trigger and reveal your values. Where money may be valued in our younger adulthood, you may come to value time over money as you age. It is also okay to not always know what values are guiding your decisions in the moment. However, the more aware of your values you can become, the more you will allow them to be the powerful, steady guardrails that guide your direction forward.

Beliefs Determine Behavior

You never have a behavior problem with your staff; you have a belief problem. Once a month, all new Providence Care employees from across the state would spend the first four hours of their career journey training with me. I wanted them to begin their new role with a full understanding of the *why* behind everything we did; as well as become immersed in the language, values, and beliefs that formed our culture. I found it extremely important to set the foundation up front about who we were.

To drive home the point that our beliefs are always the underlying driver of behavior, one of the first questions I would always ask the group was what time we were all supposed to be at work. Without fail, everyone would say nine o'clock. Then, having established the fact that everyone was aware and knew the expectation, I would ask, "So who was here the earliest?" There would always be one or two who said they had shown up ten or fifteen minutes early. After commending them, I would then ask who arrived the latest—looking around the room with a smile and a wink, to let them know that no one was in trouble. Eventually, and reluctantly, someone would raise their hand and say they were five, six, or even eight minutes late. I thanked the brave soul for admitting it and then asked them why. They knew the expectation of being there at nine, so why were they late? I heard all the typical reasons one might expect. Someone's daughter had been slow to brush her teeth, traffic had been very slow on Highway 85, or someone forgot their cell phone on the kitchen table and had to run back to get it. All legitimate and great reasons. Life happens, right? To prove my point regarding beliefs, I would then ask the team what would have happened if I had called or texted them the night before and told them that the first one to arrive at the meeting would receive $10,000 in hundred dollar bills. I then asked the tardy person what would have changed in their behavior if that was the case. Would they have made it to work on time? They immediately responded with confidence and commitment with a resounding *yes*. But what about her daughter and traffic? What about leaving the cell phone behind? Life would still have happened, but their preparation for it would have changed.

When you believe something is important enough, your behavior changes, and as the beliefs grow bigger, so too does your commitment. If a smoker believed without a shadow of a doubt that their next cigarette would be the one and final smoke that would induce the deadly heart attack, would their addiction potentially disappear? I believe it could, assuming they wanted to live. Clearly defined beliefs set the standards of behavior—for yourself and for those around you. Beliefs fused with passion dictate behavior, serving as the song sheet that everyone can play from, in unison.

Building your culture from your beliefs is about attempting to capture the common thread in the sentiments shared by team members. It's about giving them a name—making them something tangible that informs how people think, speak, and act going forward. They become the compass used by everyone to navigate the waters of decision. When you believe something, you are likely going to act on it. Also, when your beliefs are clear, you eliminate the potential distractions of misaligned beliefs. Once beliefs are firmly established, your work becomes a matter of who is committed to your culture and who is not. When you encourage an alignment with your beliefs, unwanted behaviors often take care of themselves. Align your beliefs and you automatically align all behaviors and collective action. You won't likely have to keep going back to fix things as you go or spend countless hours wondering why things aren't working. Instead, you can rally a group of people from any background around common beliefs and core values.

Your beliefs provide the standard by which you operate. It is one you can use to qualify others to join your endeavor, whether you are hiring within an organization, building out a community, or teaching children what you believe matters. Just as you can interview those in an existing organization or community, to find out what they believe, you can do the same for yourself. As it concerns the vision you want to achieve:

Take stock:

- *What do you believe about yourself, your family, your teammates, or your organization?*
- *What does excellence look like as you begin progressing toward the fulfillment of your vision?*
- *To what standards do you hold yourself accountable and why?*
- *What is your definition of exceptional teamwork and what does that look like?*

Observe trends:

- *What is working? What is not?* Write these trends down and use them as a template for how you want to do things going forward. People are people, and our lives typically boil down to similar wants, needs, and desires. Great leaders understand the value in observation and taking note of what is working and what needs some extra TLC.

Bigger organizations get this wrong too often. They think if they just train more, they will get the results they want. Wrong! By itself, training will never be enough to predict outcomes. When you are building a team, a community, or an enterprise, identifying your beliefs will fly in the face of training and education. Beliefs provide an organic recursive training. Build a team that is all singing from the same song sheet and there will be far fewer bumps in the road as you progress forward. Take your answers to these questions to heart. Post them somewhere that will remind you of what you are aiming to build. See them as targets for you and all those you will be teaming up with. Let them be what you aspire to achieve. Congruence with your values means you are living and working within the boundaries of who you say you are. Living with this kind of integrity will give you the confidence to progress forward.

Use Your Language as Leverage

If you want to change how you feel about your work, change the language you use when you are working! At Providence Care, I intended to have our philosophy revolve around slowing down and taking the necessary time to truly connect with those we served. We'd meet our patients where they were and figure out what they truly needed. Our most pressing question would always be, "How can we give you your best day today?" In order to empower this process, I wanted to take the typical, lazy industry language and make it impactful to our unique culture and mission. For instance, the standard phrase "working *on* something" would become "working *toward* something." It was a change in language that would ensure we were focusing on results, not just tasks. Instead of asking patients to "*sign* something" (because signing anything feels like you're giving away power), we would instead change the word and ask them to "*approve* their care plans." The change in language allowed them to be reminded that they remained in control of decisions.

Far too many teams and enterprises feel as though they have a *communication* problem, when what they really have is a *language* problem! In any aspect of life—within a company, a community, or your family—you may find yourself struggling to hear others or to be heard. Why? Because while you and others may be familiar with one another and use the same words, you are often referencing different dictionaries to define them! The weight of our personal perspectives can give unintended meaning to our words or how they are received. I could say "like," but you reference it as "love." You could ask for something "now," but I could understand it to mean within the next hour. When my eight-year-old daughter, Zoe, says that I "never" let her friends sleep over, that word brings with it a certain feeling of finality, which in reality is not true. When I ask her to restate it as truth, she clarifies that I "sometimes" don't let her friends sleep over. The change of wording immediately changes the emotions and the feelings behind how the *no* was experienced. When you are not speaking the same language and can't understand one another, the default setting for your communication will always be division. How you feel, as well as the quality of your life, will always be impacted. In order to foster a cohesive culture that lasts, you must speak the same language—a language of cohesion, accuracy, and success.

Language produces the feeling that dictates behavior, which in turn influences culture. Everything you intend your culture to be, based on the beliefs you have outlined, will either be forged or forgotten based on the language you use. It's that simple. When you are speaking something, you are likely doing it! That's why your cultural beliefs can't simply be a poster on a wall; they need to be demonstrated as the language that comes out of your mouth and as something everyone on your team can *feel*. Everyone also needs to understand this language rooted in your beliefs.

Here are some points for directing your language and ensuring it is fueling the belief-based culture you intend to create:

- **Start by stopping:** Any time you want to move forward, start by stopping to assess where you currently are. Take inventory by evaluating what you have said to others over the course of a day or week. *How are you presenting things to yourself and others? What state are you in and what state are you creating?*
- **Halt disempowering talk:** *What words are you speaking that are not providing positive reinforcement or encouragement? Can you replace those words with others that are more accurate to what you believe?*
- **Read it to feel it:** There is power when reading something aloud, as it allows us to really try language on and see how it feels. Use this method to assess whether certain language is beneficial and impactful, or not. *How do the words feel in your body?* Use this principle in terms of how you speak to yourself, as well as how you communicate with others.

- **Maintain sensitivity:** In working with others and empowering their language, be sensitive to where people are. Meet them where they are. Learning a new language of any kind takes time. Use the bond you have forged with your team and stakeholders, through your shared beliefs, as the foundation for encouraging the new language.

The quality of your life will be equal to the quality of the words you use. If today *sucks* because you were late to work, that will give you a totally different feeling than if today was really *inconvenient* because you were late to work. A single word can change the entire feeling of a conversation, and that feeling can change the quality of your life. When everyone is talking the same way, using positive, progressive language, your culture will organically strengthen. Things will begin to flow. For this reason, it is critical that you are always intentional about the words you use; lay the foundation of your team or enterprise language *before you begin to hire*. Doing so will help reduce confusion and enhance cohesion. Build your business, team, or community around empowering language, founded in your beliefs, and you will forge the culture you intend to create.

The Key Questions

Build from Beliefs

- Align Vision to Values:
    - *How many people's lives were made better because you got out of bed? What values are driving this impact?*
    - *What is the anticipated/ideal result when your vision is fully executed? Does it fully align with your values? If not, what needs to shift?*
- Beliefs Determine Behavior:
    - *Is life happening for you or against you?* This fundamental belief will influence every question you ask yourself from this point forward.
    - *When you look at yourself or those around you, what beliefs can you see influencing your behaviors? Which ones need to change?*
- Use Your Language as Leverage:
    - *When you use certain words, does it leave you feeling better or worse? Do your chosen words exaggerate the situation in any way, distorting your experience of it? How does doing so impact the quality of your life and the lives of others?*
    - *What empowering words can you begin to use more often? What disempowering words can you wean from your vocabulary?*

Take Action

1. **Give it a short and sweet meaning:** Make your core values five items or less, with each of them centering around the core aspects of the enterprise or team you are leading.
2. **Welcome a diversity of beliefs** (on how to achieve your vision, *not* on what your vision is): The healthy conflict found with open debates and perspective-sharing can help refine and expand the beliefs that lie at the foundation of your culture. That said, you never want to be left debating your ultimate desired outcome. Your vision must stand firm to avoid confusion and disarray.
3. **Do the next right thing that is true to your values:** With every action you take, ask yourself: *Does what you are doing align with your values? Or is it helping to reveal a new belief?* Don't let a day go by that you didn't progress towards your goal and do it always in alignment with the core beliefs you have established. Keep executing on that next thing that brings you one step closer to the fulfillment of your vision, while staying true to what matters. This will help reinforce your culture every day.
4. **Mind your words:** Think about what actions you want to see happen and put them into words! Begin with the outcome in mind yet again. Since language sets the foundation for culture, you need to always be

cognizant of your words and how they are landing with others. *What words are reinforcing your culture and which ones are pushing against it?*

As you begin setting the foundation and developing your culture, don't be surprised when it proves to be more difficult to accomplish than you originally thought. As new personalities come into the mix, your core beliefs will be tested over and over again. Whatever you are building will continue to develop as you grow. This does not mean that it will change so much as it will become enhanced. That's because it cannot do so without your core beliefs changing.

Just remember that there is a difference between something that's hard because you are growing into who you want to become and something that's hard because it's fake and misaligned with what you stand for! You will never be able to act outside of your core values and principles for long, because you will begin to feel an incongruence with who you truly are. Forge ahead in misalignment, and when you finally let go from your grasp, the pendulum will swing so far back that you may find yourself having to start anew. This will happen because you have been denying yourself the opportunity to be who you truly are and honor the beliefs that matter most to you. You will have deprived yourself of your true identity.

TRUST
THE JUMP

In every day, in some small way, you should be growing toward your goal.

MILESTONE 4:
ALIGN YOUR ASSETS

ALIGN YOUR ASSETS

At one of the Rock Hill high schools in South Carolina, I was called in to speak to the student members of a leadership development club as part of their monthly meeting. My intent was to share with them about the elements of leadership and the essential keys to entrepreneurship. Standing before the group, one of the first things I did was take a crisp, twenty dollar bill out of my wallet and asked, "Who would like twenty dollars?" Almost everyone's hands instantly jutted into the air. After a ten-second pause as everyone's hands remained raised, I asked once again. "Who would like twenty dollars?" Giggles started to echo throughout the auditorium, as students began looking at each other. Nothing else had changed. After a third attempt of asking the very same question with a little extra intonation and volume added to my voice, a young woman made her way down from the safety of the crowd and with a sheepish smile reached out and quickly snatched the bill from my hand. I asked for her name and posed one simple question. Could she please tell her friends why she currently had twenty dollars, and they didn't? Her answer seemed obvious and simple. "Because I got up and took it!" she said. Yes, she had been the one to stand up and take action.

Your ability to take focused and consistent action toward your goal is more important than any other single talent you may have. Most of us are familiar with the Pareto Principle, better known as the 80/20 rule, whereby eighty percent of our effects stem from just twenty percent of our actions. From my experience, I have reframed this principle to state that at least eighty percent of your success will be dependent upon taking consistent action—the twenty percent. Progress is about more than awareness. Not only do you need to know what actions to take, but you must know in what order to take them. It's truly the difference between doing good things versus doing the right things. If luck is where preparation meets opportunity, you must say that young lady with a new twenty dollar bill in her pocket was lucky because she took the right action at the right opportunity. This is the essence of success.

When you want to stand out and fulfill your goal, you must be willing to go beyond the status quo. Welcome to your point of leaning fully into your faith. Having set the foundation for your work by clarifying your vision, knowing what is guiding you, and building a culture from beliefs, it is now time to launch! As you do, the first challenge you encounter will be an immediate test of whether or not you truly believe in what you have established. It is a calling that can be answered by your willingness to take action. Whether you are called to become an entrepreneur, step into a new leadership role, or are already heading a team or enterprise, your belief in your vision is going to be tested and proven through your ability to consistently *do something.*

Until now, you've been thinking about and talking about your vision; now is the time to take the first steps. Now is the time where you lay friction to your faith. That is what "aligning your assets"—milestone four—is all about. Before you expand your dream to a team or dive into selling, this is where you must begin.

Your launch will begin with a detailed inventory of the team and resources you will need and those you currently have at your disposal. In this next phase of your journey to disrupting failure, you will begin to invest in resources and rally a team around your goal. It's time to pick up the phone, have the meeting, and establish the connections! Things are about to become a lot more real, quickly, as you determine how things will come together to support your vision. You may feel as though you are standing at the base of the mountain by yourself, but pay attention to the fact that even though you may not see it all before you in this moment, you are definitely not alone! What you need in order to climb the proverbial mountain are four main components:

- **The Team**: Who will you recruit to join you?
- **The Time**: Everyone has the same amount of time, although not all of us maximize it. How can you best use this gift?
- **The Money**: Think beyond dollars and cents. When you need finances, expand your definition to include other currency at your disposal: what opportunities are there to bring in talent, trade, credit, or even equity?

- **Your Desire:** The most powerful resource, one that not everyone considers, may be your most powerful weapon: you! You are the secret sauce needed to pull all of the other resources together in the highest possible capacity.

When your goal is the fulfillment of your vision, you cannot afford to sit around and wait for a knock at the door or for the phone to ring. How are you going to go about doing what is required? What team and resources are going to help you get to where you need to be? Time, people, and money—these resources will play varying amounts of importance as you progress forward toward success. Your eyes must remain wide open to take note of current resources, as well as what you are going to need and when. Is it more time, more money, or more talent? One of the greatest resources that I had at the time of my launch was time—time to contemplate and make the best resource decisions possible. I did not have to worry any longer about working forty or fifty hours a week for someone else. I could focus solely on my dream.

Without the red tape of being an established organization, you too may have been gifted the speed, agility, and a lack of barriers to move forward as needed. It's truly up to you to determine which resources serve as the required prescription for your present needs—as you launch and at every point in time going forward.

The Team

Within three weeks of launching Providence Care, I had secured my operating license from the state. It was then time to staff the company with those who could start doing the work. The problem was that I didn't know how I was going to do it, because the numbers weren't adding up. When the *why* of what you want to accomplish is big enough, you don't stop until the *how* shows up! With a lack of significant financial resources, I put myself on a budget, deprived myself of my daily coffee indulgence at Dunkin', and started calling everyone I knew who might be willing to help out with talent, time, or money. Humility became my closest ally, as I began to ask others to help. Finding anyone willing or able to invest was difficult, as was identifying those who would be willing to work for a cause that represented far more than a paycheck.

I was also in immediate need of a part-time nurse. My thoughts immediately went to Gerry, a sixty-eight-year-old veteran hospice care provider who had amassed more knowledge about helping patients than I could ever hope to learn. She had worked with me at Hallmark and had just retired earlier that year. When I called to tell her about starting my own company, she immediately told me about how much she hated retirement. And so, I offered to take her to lunch, where I asked if she'd be willing to help. I promised I would pay her after we started making money, and that that was the best I could do. I will never forget the love and grace in her eyes when she looked at me from across the table and said, "Well Johnnie, you know I am on Social Security, and I can only make a certain amount without it hurting my benefit. Since you can't afford to pay me, and I can't afford to make any additional money, why don't I just work for free and you pay me what you can when you can?"

As the *how* to my *why* was becoming clearer, what unfolded could never be detailed in a business plan. Forty-five days after I had been fired from Hallmark, I had a license from the Department of Health, allowing us to provide care to the few initial patients we could afford to treat and a nurse who was willing to work for free. I stood in awe. Thirty days after receiving my license, Dr. Romin called me up. He too had been fired from Hallmark, and he wanted us to start the company together. As a doctor, he could address the gap of my not being able to directly work with patients. As an added bonus, he was willing to match my initial investment.

Providence had truly begun to show up on all fronts. Together, we quickly found alignment in wanting to run a clean business in service to changing patient lives, where our strengths would balance out our weaknesses. We joked about how I wouldn't pretend to be a doctor if he wouldn't pretend to be an entrepreneur, and with a handshake, he began to write the prescriptions, and I began to write the checks.

Life is a team sport; an army of one will always be easily defeated. Anything that is worth doing requires the help of other people. There are only so many hours in a day that you can personally pour into building your vision and only so much energy you can give alone. As you stand at the base of the mountain with possibility in your mind's eye, who are you going to surround yourself with to help make your vision a reality? Beginning to build your team is about putting faces and names to the gaps that you need to fill. Do so by asking yourself:

- *Who are the players—the family members, friends, neighbors, coaches, mentors, employees, or employers who are best suited and willing to help?*
- *Who are those who are clearly aligned with your vision, motivations, and beliefs?*
- *Who will help you take that first step? Who will be there for the second and third?*

This stage is about shaping a tribe that supports each other. Think about what you can envision things becoming when you bring on the right people! Begin with proximity—those closest to you. As with Dr. Romin and Gerry, building a team starts with bringing on the one person who can help offset your weakness. As with any great partner, make sure you identify specific roles and responsibilities clearly. From there, you can build around that one person, bringing on more individuals who have the skills and abilities you don't have. Just remember that who you start your team with may not be who you finish with. That is okay, and sometimes preferable, based on their skillsets.

In starting Providence, I had to quickly transition my thinking from believing I could do things alone to building teams around me that serve in specific areas of my life: financial teams, spiritual teams, lifestyle teams, and health teams, for example. It's your time to ask who is best suited to join forces with you to fulfill your vision. Qualify potential team members by asking the following questions:

- *Do they have the hard talent or ability that you need?*
- *Who are they and what are their desires?*
- *Who do they want to become?* Practically speaking, most people coming into business are looking for a paycheck, but work will always ultimately be the pursuit of becoming who we want to become.
- *Are they aligned with where you are going? Do they have the same standards and beliefs?* When you answer the above question, you get clarity of whether someone wants to become aligned with your beliefs.

In the beginning, many people will want you to succeed, because they find what you are doing to be admirable. When you approach others with humility, a willingness to learn, and your heart in the right place, chances are you will make progress in building the right team.

Building your resources is about getting others excited in your vision. However, remember that while you may be looking at how they can support you with your vision, it is equally important to question how you are going to support them in whatever they envision for themselves! It has to be a two-way street. At the root of any worthwhile pursuit, you and the team are ultimately taking this action to pursue common vision. We are all in search of a better tomorrow, for oneself *and* for others. Stay creative, open-minded, and resourceful; look to the spaces in between for potential resources, and ask yourself where there may be support that you may not currently see. Opportunity lies everywhere when you have the eyes to see it.

The Time

All too often, time can become a wasted resource. However, when you focus in on time, you can really exploit it. If you are an entrepreneur beginning a business, for example, chances are you currently have an imbalance between time and money. There is not yet enough money coming in, and you find yourself with an abundance of time—to network and build relationships, to study, to test your vision, to make the necessary adjustments, and to get out there and work your tail off. While it can feel as though there is only so much you can do while waiting on external factors—the loan, the ideal teammates, etc.—you can't let time just pass you by! Use it as leverage. Every day, in some small way, be growing toward your goal. Use your time to help prepare for the point of when the green flag waves, and your engine is primed, you are ready to go.

When it comes to maximizing your time, ask yourself:

- *What can you do today to get you one step closer to your goal?*
- *What is time granting you the unique opportunity to do or become* (that you wouldn't do if you were too busy with something else)?
- *What conversation could I be having today? Who will bring me one inch closer?*

Winning or losing does not come at the end of the month, the quarter, or the year; *it happens every single day.* Ask better questions and you'll get better answers! Ponder these questions daily and you will continuously push yourself one step closer to your goal. Measure daily progress with ten minutes of what I call "ceiling fan moments"—time when you are lying in bed, looking up at the fan (or the light), taking the moment to summarize your day. Did you do everything possible? Did your choices bring you closer to the fulfillment of your vision, or did they take you further from it? Write out the details of your day's actions and the results. So many aspects of what you need to do are just about having reoccurring conversations, asking, and finding ways to create value to fulfill other's needs. Did you achieve that? If not, you missed an opportunity that you cannot afford to miss. You need to adjust tomorrow.

Time is always offering you an opportunity to line everything up and keep striving for consistent and limitless improvement. It gives you the chance to strengthen your foundation, to ensure you have chosen the right season and cycle. Use it to know if you've had the right conversations and used the right language. Determine exactly where you want and need to be when the light turns green. Time is offering you the gift of focus and the ability to slow down to not be as distracted by other things. Choosing to make the most of it is like lining up and pulling a slingshot back. Then, when you are ready to go, the impact of your actions will be further reaching. They will be lined up to disrupt failure at all points.

The Money

Our economy moves on dollars—the exchange of one element of value for another. Being at a point where you are seeking monetary resources means you have reached the point where your vision begins to cost you something. In order to make progress, everything you do at this stage needs to be an investment—a return on your dollar and a catalyst to the successful fulfillment of a vision. Not a dime can be wasted or frivolous. This will require sacrifice and outside-the-box thinking.

Everyone has the same amount of time, but not everyone has the same amount of money. No matter how hard you sell your vision, no one is going to care about what you are creating more than you do! In order to procure everything you know you need, it is necessary to know how much that is and by when. You also have to allow yourself the freedom to be creative and resourceful. As you identify what monetary resources you have, need, and can exchange something for, ask yourself:

- *How much do you truly need and by when?*

- *How much do you currently have to allocate to launching your vision?*
- *What is the difference between what you have and what you need?*
- *Where can you begin to source support to fill this gap?*

When starting Providence Care, the industry dictated that a half-million dollars was the sum required to purchase the team, beds, wheelchairs, medical equipment, oxygen tanks, and pharmaceutical supplies needed to begin treating patients. It was $133 per day, per patient, to operate and break even. Raising the amount required to properly launch the endeavor was financially impossible, and time was not on my side. Instead of attempting to surmount the near-impossibility of finding half a million dollars immediately (without selling out ownership of the company), I chose to reframe the question. What could I create starting with the $50,000 Dr. Romin and I were willing to invest?

As I waited for my license, I began relentlessly asking for help. My first call was to my local pharmacy, where the owner knew how I did business and that I paid my bills. This was where my reputation would either be a huge benefit or a liability. Positioning myself as a new, long-term customer for the pharmacy, and explaining my vision, I told him I needed twelve months of patient support and had no way to pay for it. On the spot, he said *yes* to an interest-free line of credit for up to a year. My medical equipment supplier agreed to do just the same, based on nothing more than a shared vision and a handshake. What was a small sacrifice for them was a huge need fulfilled for us.

The crux of everything you need to launch your vision is leveraging relationships where you have them and continuing to ask for what you need. Do this by selling your vision and offering value to others first. An ask for money is really about asking someone to help you when it's in their best interest to do so. Aim to bring so much value that it becomes an easy *yes* for them. As you evolve and find greater comfort in the asking process, you can change your approach as needed to further clarify the value you are bringing to those who decide to ride with you.

It is crucial to think beyond money being currency alone; it is much bigger than that! It is the exchange of one thing of value for another. Remember that it always has to come down to creating value for others first. When you are seeking the financial resources you need, look at what you have of value that can be exchanged for something that is of value to someone else. Is it labor, volunteerism, a tax write-off, or something else?

When starting out, you will not be able to compete from a monetary perspective. This means that sometimes you must compete by being resourceful! I got what I needed to start Providence Care by relying on my ability to connect with others on a personal level and sell them on the vision of serving an underserved population. The agreements became about them seeing themselves as the type of people who wanted to have a stake in helping us save lives and overserve the underserved. This was also their chance to make a big impact with very little risk. The focus was both on the short-term help that Providence Care needed, but more importantly, it was on their opportunity for a long-term, mutually beneficial relationship.

Your Desire

For the first six months after launching Providence Care, I didn't leave my house between the hours of 8:00 AM and 5:00 PM.

Regulations stated that the office had to be open for that exact window, Monday through Friday (and at the time, my house *was* the office, and we couldn't afford to hire staff to be present in my absence). Second, if I wanted things to get off the ground, I had no choice but to wait for Medicare to arrive and conduct the surprise survey we needed to get reimbursed for patient care. We had fulfilled all of the Conditions of Participation (CoPs) requirements and submitted our notice to receive one of the standard unannounced assessments. Medicare had ninety days to complete the survey—a review that would have two federal officials go through every chart we had on file, check on patients who had passed away, verify all regulations, and do ride-alongs with nursing staff, all over the course of three days. For everything they found to be done incorrectly (the tags), we would have to create a Plan of Correction and submit it to the government, giving them another thirty to forty-five days to approve our plan so we could start billing Medicare.

As I waited for them to arrive, I didn't know how much longer we could stretch out the $50,000 Romin and I had invested. By this point, we were down to pennies. All I had was my small team, my time, and a willingness to take the hits and get back up, to adjust, and to become more flexible. We were feeling the weight of serving our current patients out-of-pocket, and time was running out. We needed the survey completed, and we needed to pass on our first shot.

On April 9, 2011, the eighty-ninth day of their ninety-day window, Medicare showed up to conduct our qualification survey. They sent in two middle-aged women, one of whom couldn't stop talking about her grandkids and the other who was infatuated with the glorious wonders of a new craze, Groupon.

As they took out their documentation and readied themselves to begin the review process, they were quickly pulled away to take a phone call. It was their home office in Columbia, South Carolina, and there was a problem. President Obama's government was on the brink of a potential shutdown amid the lingering fragility from the economic recovery following the 2008 crash. This would have suspended over 800,000 federal workers, and the Medicare team to be unable to complete our survey. They would need to finish our three-day review in just a single day. What were the chances of such a blessing during a time where their shortened window could bring us two days closer to earning income?

Both women were very kind, though the moment they sat down at the dining room table to get to work, their backs straightened as they began to sternly check the boxes on their forms. Knowing the financial pressure Providence was facing, I immediately began selling them on the vision for what we were trying to do. To my great surprise, it quickly became clear that despite their sometimes-rigid professionalism, both of them were willing to help us through the process. As we progressed through the company's numbers, they gave me the opportunity to correct discrepancies on the spot.

Providence Care ended up with a one-hundred-percent deficiency-free survey, and the two women left—but only after hugging me and showing me pictures of their children and grandchildren. While they may not have realized it, from the moment they stepped in the door, they had become part of Providence Care's legacy. It felt as though the right people had walked through my door that day. I called Romin and excitedly told him we had passed. Now we could build our team, begin making money, and start impacting more lives.

Your profits will equal your passion. The fourth resource that most people don't think about is *you*! As a leader, you are responsible for everything that comes behind you. In any resource-based decisions, you get to control what you are giving away and what you are accepting. Believe in yourself and become a 24/7 walking billboard for what you want to create! Everywhere, at every moment, you need to look for an opportunity to share and act upon your vision. Most people want to be and do something greater than themselves, but they have not yet found a clear vision for themselves or the motivation required to obtain that vision. Capitalize on that!

All of the resources you can gather will come down to your passion and desire. You are the driving force behind gathering everything you require. It is going to be inevitable that you'll be knocked down and have to get back up again. You are going to be told *no* or run into stop signs. This will require an unbridled tenacity and the need to get creative and keep trying different approaches, until you get your *yes*. Assume the best, even when questions remain as to where your required resources are going to come from, and then keep forging ahead until you realize success. This is going to be the story of your tenacity. Have the flexibility to pivot and change your approach. Keep pushing, even when things seem impossible, and forge new relationships, as needed to acquire necessary resources.

The Key Questions

Align Your Assets

- The Team:
    - *Do they have the desire?* In addition to ensuring you have directional alignment, you want your teammates to love what you are doing as much as you do.
- The Time:
    - *Did you make progress today? Why or why not?*
    - *What did you procrastinate on or make excuses for? How did that set you back?*
- The Money:
    - *What do you have that's of value that others may be willing to exchange for something that is of value to you?*
- Your Desire:
    - *What did you do today to bring yourself one step closer to your goal?*
    - *What worked in the past that you can do again? What did right look like?*

Take Action

1. **Identify your one:** In the infancy stage, you will start out small. You won't need twenty or a hundred players. Begin by identifying that first critical team member who will be there for the initial steps. Who will offset or augment the skillset or abilities you don't have? Build around that person.
2. **Look for trends:** When it comes to how you are using your time, look for past trends to improve upon or take advantage of. What has worked that you can repeat? Are there any areas where you need to change your approach?
3. **When it comes to seeking financial resources, remain open-minded and creative:** Instead of asking for generic support, be specific enough that someone knows the opportunity they are signing up for. And always remind them what's in it for them!
4. **Create connection to your vision:** Finding the right people is about bringing in those who adopt your vision as part of their own. Attach their heart to your vision, in order to make it undeniably attractive.

There will never be a better tomorrow if you are comfortable enough to stay still and simmer in the status quo. As you take your leap of faith, there are days that will be nice, although the norm is going to be one of hard work and frustration. When you are striving to grow, you need to continuously keep moving forward, using your time wisely and building your resources. Through different seasons, certain resources will play bigger roles than others. Your needs for a team, your time, or the money will fluctuate. What matters is the pursuit of continuous movement and growth, because you can't move forward or disrupt failure by staying where you have always been. Reach out and grab that twenty-dollar bill! As you start to progress in the execution of your vision, you are going to begin to feel the shackles on your feet—those that were previously holding you back. When you do, don't be surprised. You are only feeling them because you are trying something new. That should be celebrated.

The launch is where many people stop or quit, because they can't move from the *why* to the *how* of their vision—a point that will be challenging and stubborn. You have to be willing to put in the work without knowing the full scope of what things will become and often without seeing immediate results. Every day is an opportunity to assess whether you have taken one step closer or one step further away from your goal. Don't be afraid to pause and take stock, in order to appreciate every ounce of momentum. Your success at this stage will be measured in inches, not miles. Stay encouraged.

“HR” does not stand for human resources; it stands for *human relationships*.

Your team may be a resource, but nurturing the relationships will always be what matters most.

MILESTONE 5: EXPAND THE DREAM TO A TEAM

EXPAND THE DREAM TO A TEAM

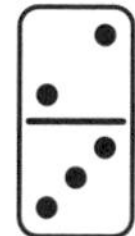

Imagine finding yourself frustrated with the two-party system of U.S. politics and deciding to start your own party. How would you move forward with such a notion? Standard procedure might dictate that you would post your vision on job sites and begin looking through the lists of credentials on the resumes of those expressing interest in building such a vision with you. In scanning applicants, you may look for pedigree, experience, abilities, talents, and the schools where candidates received their degrees. Yet, would you look for or question what they believe? If not, why not?

When you think about it, how far would you really progress in growing your vision of a revolutionary new party if you ended up with a communist, a totalitarian, a capitalist, and a socialist rounding out your team? Despite your clear vision for what you want to create, how long would it take for a team with such differing ideologies and perspectives to come together and align? How long would it take for them to find common ground and move the needle forward? It would likely end up with a result similar to that of starting a new religious movement with a team made up of Agnostics, Christians, and Wiccans. The hard truth is that full agreement is unlikely, because those you have brought together to form your team do not believe the same thing.

Inherently, we know that a team made up of differing beliefs and ideologies would be completely dysfunctional, yet this is exactly how many organizations hire and recruit every day! They look for competency and ignore compatibility, and then wonder why they have dysfunction. You can bring on the most intelligent candidates, with degrees from the best Ivy League institutions, but without alignment of vision and beliefs, you lack the foundation for success. When your team isn't all going in the same direction and believing in it, you will risk sabotaging each other. Their respective missions will never lead you to collectively make it to the top of the mountain.

Pulling together an ideal team, composed of cohesion and camaraderie, means creating an environment where clarity of vision rules over confusion. There must be a complete sense of belonging and trust—a true goodwill relationship among all team members. There will always be an element of inconsistency and personality sprinkled into the mix, and you may not agree with what each member says or does, but in the ideal team environment, you can trust that everyone's motivations are good and their values are aligned. You know this because you did the foundational work up front—to establish your core values before bringing on a team! With the foundation set, you are ready to hire, develop, train, and retain the best talent.

- **Recruit:** Ideal hires will have much more than the certifications, skills, and training required to fulfill a role; they will have a vision and beliefs that align with yours.
- **Develop and Train:** Create the environment where every member of your team can thrive. Training builds the thought processes required to solve problems. It leads your team where they want to go, until they have arrived.
- **Retain:** Check in with your team members regularly and offer support with their current needs and future career visions. Be the one to answer the questions *where are we today* and *where are we going*?

If you're ready, let's dive into milestone five and explore how to best expand your dream into a team.

Recruit

When I began interviewing candidates to join Providence Care, I wanted to rally together people with a willingness to help patients who needed it the most. As I would sit with candidates, I would work toward qualifying whether they were a good fit for our culture by painting a scenario for them. Many times, I would try to talk them out of the job, just to see if they would bite. I would describe to them, in detail, how many of our patients' unkempt homes were infested with fleas and roaches, in less-than-ideal neighborhoods, and without air conditioning in the heat of summer. The conditions would be nothing like the comfortable, climate-controlled hospitals where they may have previously served! Why would they want to put themselves in such conditions to take care of the patient? Did they really earn their degree or certificate to have to endure this? What each candidate told me next would tell me everything I needed to know. A willingness to step into a situation of discomfort to support a patient in need would clearly depict their ability to willingly serve the underserved, without discrimination or exemption. It would tell me that our vision and values were aligned in relation to at least one of our core values; *we are where they are.*

What benefit is the most impressive credentials when there is no alignment of values and vision? What good is it to have all the greatest moral and ethical attributes without the energy to get out of bed in the mornings and use them? At the end of the day, the hiring process is about finding team members who have a true *wow factor* about them. You want to hire those who also have the enthusiasm to give of their substance and talents, adding to the cohesion of your team. It's about looking for what I like to call *the salt and pepper* in a candidate. Pepper is what I see as the spice of life—the passion and zeal you expect employees to have. Salt is the essence of the person—who and what they are at their core. A candidate can have all the degrees, know all the right people, and possess all the right skills far above what the job requires; but when they don't have *both* salt and pepper, it can quickly become a fatal flaw.

There are three key areas on which you must focus your hiring process to ensure you find the salt and pepper your team requires:

1. **Align a candidate's personal visions with where you want to go:** Job seekers don't care about your job description; they care about the story and the adventure it holds for them. In order to achieve alignment of vision, it's the responsibility of leadership to lay out

clearly not only what the organization is but also where it came from. Help new hires understand what they have been hired to achieve! Alignment of vision is achieved when you don't hire people solely based on what they can do today, but rather, what they can do to help catapult where you want to be in the future.

Center your hiring process around the question *how can I help you become more of who you want to be?* More specifically, ask potential hires:

- *Where do they want to go?*
- *What is already within them that is aligned with what you want to do?*
- *What are their hopes, dreams, and desires?*

Establish expectations as to what they will become in their role and what the organization will be for them. Interview for the journey, not the job, and always *hire for tomorrow.*

2. **Synergy with culture and core beliefs:** With all the thoughts and efforts you put into creating a culture based on beliefs, the hiring process will provide one of the greatest tests of its realization and sustainability. A diversity of opinions and backgrounds can help an enterprise thrive, although the clashing of core beliefs can sink a mission. A candidate can be heading in the same direction as you and your vision, although that doesn't mean anything when your beliefs are not

aligned! Your core values establish a standard to hold others to, making them the qualifying criteria for selecting candidates who align. The bigger-picture questions you need to have answered within your interviews are:

- *What is their core belief system? Does it match the organization's (or is it even better)?*
- *What is their work ethic and philosophy for rendering service?*
- *What are the standards they hold themselves to (even when no one is looking)? Do they meet the standards of your organization?*

When a candidate does not share your core values, standards, or passions, don't hire them. It's as simple as that. If you ignore this golden rule, you will likely be bound for constantly putting out fires and dealing with endless behavioral problems.

3. **Blend hard skills and soft skills:** While pedigree (required certifications, skills, and technical degrees) is necessary, it should follow only after alignment of vision and beliefs has been met. Assessing a candidate's fit has to be about what you will need them to do (hard skills) and how they go about doing it (soft skills)! When assessing your initial hires, you want to look for generalists (unicorns)—those who understand the broader business and can accomplish a variety of tasks

outside their departments, in addition to being specialists in their lanes. Get to know what candidates are made of by evaluating the following attributes (sprinkled with a dash of salt and pepper, of course):

- *What gets them energized? Can you harness that enthusiasm on the job?*
- *What are their talents (things that come naturally and for which they don't need to work very hard)?*
- *What are the industry-specific hard skills or certifications in play? Do they meet the basic requirements?*
- *Can they help bring you to the place that you envision going (not just sustain you in your current place)?*

While answering the above questions, you also need to consider:

- *Are they ethical?*
- *Can they handle conflict and rise above stress?*
- *Are they team players with a knack for inspiring and getting along well with others?*
- *Are they creative thinkers and natural problem-solvers?*

Before you begin, always start by asking yourself *if you truly need to hire in the first place*! It is a complete waste of time to hire when you didn't need to. How do you really know when you need to add additional staff? Here is one of the best pieces of advice I can give. Following this formula has saved me hundreds of thousands of dollars over the years. Never hire unless you ask yourself this set of questions first:

- *What is the precise problem you are trying to solve or the opportunity you are trying to seize?*
- *What would happen if you did nothing? What will the impact be on your vision, organization, team, group, or community?*
- *What technology can be implemented to fix the need and at what cost?*
- *Is there anything that you can delegate to a third-party person/vendor or outsourced to a subcontractor? Or could a volunteer or technology be brought in to address the need?*

Whether you are operating within an existing organization or starting a team from scratch, your ideal tribe will be built by picking one player at a time, always keeping your culture and values top-of-mind. At the end of the day, you want to always be recruiting. Even when you are not actively hiring, you want to be thinking about it and preparing a deep bench of great potential candidates to pull from. Hire for strengths, realizing they may be hidden in what others would call weaknesses. You can protect yourself from potential misalignment or *human relationship* struggles by having a really good hiring process in place and ensuring you always recruit out of inspiration and not desperation.

You may not be able to find the ideal people from day one. That's okay. Your hires may also not be the caliber of people you need to get to the next level, even if they can help today. You can always move to better talent when you have outgrown the abilities of some who started out with you. Right now, if you aren't able to find all of the required candidates that fully align with your vision, that too is okay. Focus on getting to the next mile marker, instead of trying to solve everything for the long-term today. Do better when you can. For instance, when you reach a point where you feel a team member's skillset feels exhausted, they will be forced to make a decision to get better or to get off the bus. Help and train where appropriate, but remain aware that you cannot afford to keep those who are unwilling to continue to grow with you.

Develop and Train

During the time I spent teaching at the Cook School of Business at Columbia International University, I addressed juniors and seniors soon to be graduating with business degrees. As in any lecture, I would walk to the front of the room, sharing a real-life perspective of hands-on business, versus simply regurgitating what they read in their textbooks. One day, I walked in with my golf bag in hand. Looking like I had somewhere else to be, I placed the bag next to me and looked out at the group. I then asked the students if they noticed anything unusual about my bag of clubs. A golfer from the college team happened to be sitting up front and immediately jumped at the opportunity to point out that the three clubs I had in my bag meant that I was missing many of the tools required to play a proper game of golf. He could clearly see that I didn't have most of my irons, my driver, or my one of my woods.

My response to the observant young golfer was this: sure, there were many tools in a full golf club set that I could be using, yet I wasn't in fact missing any of my tools. I had intentionally brought only the three clubs I was really good at. Knowing the PGA tour wasn't calling any time soon, I was confident that I could play a pretty decent golf game using just them. The moral of the story is that none of us need to know it all! When it comes to training yourself and your team, less is most often more. Development should be focused on the key tools required at the key times. Become an expert with just *three to five key tools,* and with consistency in your mastery of their use, you will thrive. This is another example of the 80/20 rule in play, where eighty percent of your success will most likely stem from twenty percent of your actions. Those actions should be centered around what every member of your team does best.

Because change today happens in an instant, not over months or quarters, you have to know your team's strengths as well as their deficits and be ready to constantly facilitate improvement. To keep pace, it is critical that you know what is evolving within your industry and what is shifting in the bigger environments that govern your work—from laws to regulations to taxation and beyond. It is also crucial to be intentional with your training. Even if you and your team feel you know it all, the environment has already changed, and you'll need to know something new tomorrow.

You always need to be learning. When your team members need to learn a new skill due to an updated procedure, an evaluation has revealed a deficiency, or you simply want to increase efficiencies in behavior, that is when you train! The training must be well thought out, developed, and always focused on the outcome you wish to achieve. Half-hearted "one and done" sessions will not cut it. Such efforts will not provide you with the foundation to navigate the twists and turns on the road ahead. To sustain growth and do things right the first time, you need to have a process—a strategy, a plan, templates, checklists, and consistent language all working to guarantee the specific outcomes you have identified. It must be centered on the vision and beliefs that lay at the foundation of your culture.

Training begins the day you hire. Answering the question, *What problem are you trying to solve or opportunity are you seizing?* should always be at the forefront and timing of your every training endeavor. When determining where the need for training lies—and prioritizing it—remember that the biggest customer you need to take care of first is the vision and mission of your entity. Before you dive into the intricacies of training and whether or not it was effective, begin by looking at things from your enterprise's perspective:

- *What are the ultimate needs of the organization today? In the next ninety days? For the next twelve months?*
- *Where do your urgent problem solving needs exist?* (Identifying the difference between urgent and important is crucial.)
- *What is the root cause of the problems or symptoms you are seeing? How can you address that through training?*
- *What are some older processes team members need to be reminded of (via retraining)? Do they need support with time management?*

- *What are some free resources or technologies you can use to offset the knowledge or skill deficit your team members may have?*

After that, you can ask more honed-in questions regarding the training needs of your individual team members:

- *What is that skill or talent that your individual team members have always been known for? How can you help grow that?*
- *Where do their natural talents lie? What are they most interested in?* (We tend to be good at the things we are most interested in.)

Train (or retrain) on the aspects of your day-to-day work—from customer service to how to best craft your email communication to how to optimize selling your product or service. Make it predictable and habitual for your team. Do this on the *same day each month.* Identify those among your people who want to learn—those who clearly want everyday improvement. Let them lead the session they are most familiar with and inspire others, while being the focus of your training efforts. When you want to get really good at training, begin picking out your key players and implementing a "train the trainer" model, where they become empowered to educate and stimulate growth for your other team members. Have your trainers develop checklists and templates first, then build a more detailed plan by creating operations manuals with every step of your training process. These all circle back to solving problems or seizing opportunities. It begins with identifying and having a conversation with your "A Players"—those who truly want to advance in their careers and who love and are proficient at teaching others.

Do your team members care enough to grow, learn, and improve? When they do, you train. When they don't, they may not be a good fit, and it may be time to part ways. In today's highly contentious marketplace, where many are competing for great talent, development is a "must have," not a "nice to have." Great team members expect it. When you are not filling that need for purpose and growth, they will find what they need with your competitor. Shape a development plan for your existing team members today, apply it, then come back in a few weeks and ask them how it went.

Training is ultimately a tool to build potential—by reminding, re-engaging, and refocusing your team—and the time to start doing it is always *now*! Even if it's not about learning something new, use training to master something old. Your team members want to know that you are investing in them and offering them more than a paycheck. Give them a greater sense of purpose by nurturing their growth (and that of your team or enterprise) through training and development. When you tap into that human need to continuously step closer to the best version of yourselves and hardwire it into your business, you will retain your people. They will be more engaged, and they will be more awake to opportunities that come knocking at your door every day.

Retain

Your team members are going to talk about each other, so why not make it a productive experience? At Providence Care, I would tell rooms full of new hires to be careful of what they did and didn't do, because we had a culture where their team members were going to talk about them behind their back! And by the way, we encouraged it. After they would look at each other and back at me with a worried expression, I'd relieve their anxiety by explaining how we loved to catch people doing something right and encouraged employees to report these acts of goodness in a forum we called "Tattle-Tale Reports." For example, a head-office team member once wrote in about how she heard a team member talking kindly to an upset patient on the phone. This person worked to solve a problem on the spot by actively listening. When they didn't know all the answers then and there, they called the patient back within half an hour with the final details. They were even late for their lunch break because of that effort. These reports, submitted in writing or electronically, allowed the team to applaud the above-and-beyond actions taken by their colleagues. They also highlighted others living the core values. It's human nature to gossip; instead of fighting that, use it to your advantage and hardwire it into your culture. Redirect negative talk into positive reinforcement, knowing that when you focus on what right looks like, you don't spend as much time on things that don't matter. The result is greater cohesion, trust, and goodwill rippling throughout the organization.

The days of people staying in one job for twenty years are gone. For most, a stint in a single role may only last a few years, less the time it takes to get settled in and learn. Interweave this with the rapid pace of change we described earlier, and you have a clear need to be strategic with how you retain team members. For sustained success, you must have an intentional recruiting process, training process, and career advancement process. When you want to create a predictable experience, you aren't going to get the desired result without doing it all by design! Retaining is about creating the habits that will support that collective success. This is built around knowing that when your team members are focused on growing and learning with you, they are incentivized to do better, be better, and to continue moving the collective mission forward.

Retaining is about building an environment where people are committed to growing themselves—having a better day today than yesterday and an even better day tomorrow—and doing it via a commitment to the needs of your team and enterprise. Without giving them what they need, your enterprise will not get what it wants! When it comes to fostering the retention of your team, always be asking yourself:

- *How can I help them form habits to create the consistent growth they need, and to become better today than they were yesterday?*
- *How can I attach it to our mission—our beliefs?*

Help your team members fulfill their need to be up to speed on the external environment and become the best they can be. Career paths, or *career ladders*, as I like to call them, can serve to keep your team members on the direction they said they want to follow. They help keep them looking to the future and moving in the direction of growth. Career ladder work should be done when a candidate is hired and then repeated annually. Focus the exercise on answering the following questions and use a template similar to the ones below:

- *Where do they want to get to in the next twelve months?*

- *What are their career wants, needs, and desires?*

CAREER LADDER

It is our commitment with all staff members to give you the tools to succeed and to help you take steps in the direction of your dreams. This tool will help us support you in your professional goals.

Name: ______________________________
Date: ______________________________

PLEASE CIRCLE 1 FOR THIS YEAR:

Rockstar: Force for stability. Ambitious outside of work or content in life. Happy in the current role. Desires growth in current position.

Superstar: Agent for change. Ambitious at work and desires more challenges. Wants new opportunities outside of current position.

CURRENT POSITION:

Desired position in 12-18 months: ________________________
Current earnings: ______________________________
Desired earnings: ______________________________
What will it mean for me / my family when I achieve it? ______
____
____

What will it mean for me / my family if I don't achieve it? _____
____
____

Realistic time frame that you are wanting to hit this goal:
____
____

Experience needed to qualify? ____________________

Education / skills needed to qualify? ________________
____

Actions I must take to reach this goal:
____

Three areas in which the organization can support you in this goal:

1. ____________________
2. ____________________
3. ____________________

Printed name: ____________________

Signature: ____________________

Review date: ____________________

Reviewing manager: ____________________

Review date: ____________________

Reviewing manager: ____________________

Review date: ____________________

Reviewing manager: ____________________

Review date: ____________________

Reviewing manager: ____________________

As an additional support for your team member's career visions, one of the best things you can do is to have daily or weekly check-ins. This is about "looking at their vitals" by asking the following questions:

- *Where are you and your team today?*
- *What did you accomplish?*
- *What went right?*
- *If you had a tool to make your job easier, what would it be?*
- *If you could remove a barrier, what would that be?*

The key to these check-ins is consistency and follow-through. Once you provide the new tool or remove the barrier, the next check-in should be an assessment for whether or not things have improved. Let team members take the lead in their growth. Be there to help guide them to where they want to go—even if they don't know that's where they want to be until they get there! This work may not feel exciting, but doing it will help you achieve forward progress with a power that makes it hard to deny success.

Building your team and helping them grow requires that you understand them, grasp their motivations, comprehend their biases, and share their visions for their careers and their future. It also means consistently soliciting feedback from across the organization. Hardwire your training processes and team member career plans into the foundation of your enterprise. This will ensure not only motivation, but also your ability to continually retain and inspire your team members. Your vision will help you recruit talent, though your culture will be what keeps them (or not). Always aim for alignment of your enterprise's vision and values with the career path of every team member. Those who are aligned don't leave!

The Key Questions

Expand the Dream to a Team

- Recruit:
    - *What are their backgrounds and motivations for wanting to join your team?*
    - *What strengths do they have that you need?*
- Develop and Train:
    - *Are your hires fit for duty? Do they have the potential, even if they don't have what you need at the moment?*
    - *What are some deficits they currently have and how can you help them get to where they need to be?*
- Retain:
    - *What are two things that would lead them to want to leave the company?* Allow them to tell you what you need to stop doing!
    - *What are the things your team/enterprise offers that you can't get anywhere else?*

Take Action

1. **Ask candidates to fix your problem:** To identify those with the ideal blend of hard and soft skills, use a "fix

my problem" scenario during interviews. This involves painting a real-world scenario for the candidate. For example, if you are hiring for a sales manager position and their target is five sales a month, though they are only doing three, what are they going to do about it? If you are hiring for an HR or team lead role, offer a scenario where one employee has just discovered that their colleague makes $2 more an hour than they do. How will they fix this problem? Create a guide of potential scenarios that stem from problems you are currently facing within your enterprise. A candidate's answers will not only show you how they think and operate; they might just provide valuable insight for fixing your current issue!

2. **Document and systemize how you train:** The keys to training are consistency and having an intentional process. Write down how you did it, how much you did, and to what degree. How often you do so will change as you identify what works and what does not. From a bigger-picture perspective, keeping track of what right looks like will ultimately become your manual for success, helping reinforce positive rituals and habits.

3. **Retain in order to sustain:** With a diverse group of individuals serving on your team, it is important to recognize and identify their personal goals and motivations—both stated and unstated. Diverse backgrounds, cultures, and personalities within the group

> allow for different values, serve different functions, and play very different roles that will dramatically affect the way the group needs to be led. Make sure their motives and aspirations remain clear (and met). Even if they choose to stay in the same lane, always help them level-up their skills to be better at what they do tomorrow. Let work be where they come to grow.

Your team members want and need mentorship, choices, room for innovation and growth, and the opportunity to become engaged. They also need clear communication, less red tape, work-life blend, and a sense of purpose and autonomy. These requirements may seem cumbersome and hard to implement, but when you get it right, you'll see many of your turnover and HR problems disappear. By helping your team members continuously step into the highest version of themselves, your success will be defined by having helped them succeed. The impact and longevity you realize for your team or enterprise will be the overflowing value you have created in shaping an environment of growth and support. It will be strengthened when you create rituals, habits, and cycles where every team member is intentionally leveling up.

Building your dream team—through strategic hiring, training, and retention processes—boils down to constantly answering one question: *How can you help each other become more of who you need to be?* When things become chaotic, you will always be there to remind them who they are and all they can become. Storms expose foundations. As a leader, it is your responsibility to be the foundation, not the roof. You are there to bear the weight and provide the stability for your team, while also hiring those who will help you further strengthen your foundation and ensure that the weight is not carried solely by you. As you are nurturing and supporting the growth of your team, remember the need to care for your team or enterprise as a whole. Human relationships are the most important thing you have, but without taking care of your mission and vision first, you won't have the foundation to support your team for the long term.

The heart comes first and then the brain follows.

Leadership is the head, but it must always be attached to the heart.

MILESTONE 6: YOU'RE SOLD, NOW GO SELL

YOU'RE SOLD, NOW GO SELL

Everything you do when interacting with others is sales, on one level or another. Consider the following scenario with respect to what you can do when challenged with the feat of selling to others.

Perhaps there was once a time when you were interviewing for a dream job. After following an organization for years and identifying with their values, all you had to do was convince the hiring manager that you were the right fit. In other words, you had to sell them on the fact that you were sold on their vision. You already understood and loved the organization. Should be an easy sell, right?

Now, imagine that the job is for a sales role at a pencil factory, and you were told by the hiring manager that if you can close a specific client, you will land the job. The client is someone the company has been trying to sell to for nearly a decade. The challenge is that the client has always bought his pencils from a family member. Your products are of the same price and quality, offer the same shipping rates, and have the very same high-quality eraser. If this wasn't enough, the next day was the client's last day before retirement. You only get one shot to make the sale. How would you do it?

In this scenario, you walk into the client's office and say, "You don't know me. I am trying to get a job with the pencil factory. Tom, the hiring manager, told me that if I can get an order from you, he is going to give me the job. He also told me that you are retiring, so congratulations on what I am sure was a great career."

As your conversation continues, you point out that the hiring manager never quantified the size of the pencil order required for him to give you the job. Perhaps you tell the prospective client, "So, if you could see your way to giving me an order for just five pencils, you could retire tomorrow with the satisfaction of knowing you finished your career by helping a young person start theirs!"

Obviously, this scenario is fictional, but did you see what happened? The sale was not about the pencil! Read that one again. All things being equal, selling others on a product, service, or idea (such as hiring you) is not about the product, service, or even the idea; it's about those you are selling seeing themselves in what you are offering. It's about building a relationship and meeting the buyer's needs or wants, not yours. When you turn the focus from the pencil to this owner's legacy in any scenario, you change your outcome. There will be no disruption to failure if you don't understand how to effectively sell. Reaching the point of persuasion in any sales process is about ultimately forming a genuine relationship and working to understand prospective customers. This is the mindset needed to build your team or enterprise from this point forward.

As the rules of free markets go, nothing is going to move without the persuasion required to exchange an idea or some kind of currency for another. Everything is sales. Whether it happens through persuasion, cooperation, or manipulation, selling is built into the human condition. Having brought on an initial team that shares in your direction and aligns with your belief-based culture, your team is likely sold on where you are going. Now, in milestone six, it's time to go get the business!

Everyone on your team has to be aligned with being an ambassador to your brand and your vision. Because you have done the foundational work up front, you have hopefully gathered a team of people who are working together toward your common mission. Your team should know they aren't there just to do a job in a silo. Regardless of title, everyone in your organization must become a walking billboard for your product or service! That's what this chapter is about: establishing a process for finding your target customer and helping you and everyone on your team confidently create value for them. If you can't sell to someone and have them engage their time, money, or some other aspect of value in exchange for your vision, you are not going to fulfill that vision.

Understand the True Sales Cycle

When launching Providence Care, I found myself on a quest to answer the question *how can I create more value than anyone else in my space?* I quickly became a walking billboard for the kind of hospice and home care I firmly believed in. Everywhere I went—from buying basic necessities at grocery stores to going out to dinner with Kelley—I couldn't keep myself from spotting opportunities to help change lives for the better. In the Walmart parking lot, Kelley would patiently wait in the car with the girls, as I felt called to approach the elderly man with his oxygen tank attempting to push his shopping cart across the parking lot. In a gentle way, I'd say, "This is none of my business, but it looks like you are having a hard time here. Can I help with your groceries or take your cart back for you?"

After giving a hand, I'd take note of his oxygen and ask if he knew that some doctors are now making house calls like they used to, as I imagined he had a hard time getting to the doctor. Their response was almost always one of agreement, which opened the door to giving them my personal cell number and telling them that I was the founder of an agency called Providence Care. It also just so happened that I always had Dr. Romin's business cards in my pocket, in case they wanted to call him to find out more regarding home care services. If Providence Care couldn't be the source of their solution, we'd help them figure out who was! These conversations were never directly about making a sale; they were founded in a genuine desire to constantly be pursuing relationships and adding value by changing lives for the better.

Building relationships and adding value as part of the sales process means that you are never setting out to get something *from* a prospective customer or referral partner. It's about wanting something better *for them*. No matter your business, you are in the service of people, helping them have a better day tomorrow! Great salespeople understand that sales boils down to relationships, versus making a quick buck. Relationships are about people and people are sales. Understanding the true sales cycle means mapping out your customer's journey and thinking about your offer from their perspective. Here is what a true relationship-building cycle should look like:

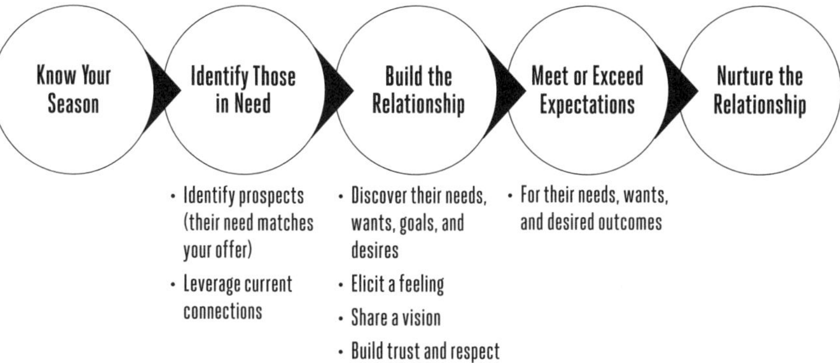

Begin by understanding what season you are in, just as you did when you questioned whether your initial vision was in season. You may find yourself in a winter season when things feel frozen. There is a great challenge to establishing new growth, and you have to rely on existing connections. Or perhaps you are in the thaw of spring, where you know it is the right time to begin planting the seeds for new sales relationships to grow. It may be summer when your prospecting efforts feel fully alive, or fall, when you are harvesting the gains from all of your relationship-building momentum.

There is something just as important as understanding the best seasons to build and harvest the gains from your sales relationships. It is being mindful that your prospective customers also have their own seasons that influence the ideal time to approach them. There will be times when your customers are more available and willing to have a conversation with you. If they are drowning in the final days of their own inventory audit or making a rapid push for their year end, it really doesn't matter what you say; your sales pitch will be out of season. Know when they are most open to hearing from you and you will increase the chances of your success.

Once you have ensured that you and your prospects are in season, you need to identify those with a need that can be met by your offer. I like to paint a "man overboard" scenario. Imagine you are enjoying the seas on your beautiful yacht, fully stocked with all the required amenities and safety gear. In the distance, you spot someone hanging onto a buoy in the water. They are so exhausted by holding on for so long, they have lost the ability to even yell for help. Do you not have a moral obligation to head their way and let them know they are seen and to offer what you can to help? What you do on those waters is the same action you need to be doing every time you see someone with a need that can be supported by your product, service, or idea.

In order to find your prospective customers, begin by thinking about the three degrees of separation (or less) between you and them. Look at the relationships and connections you have already built and identify which ones could prove beneficial as prospecting partnerships or potential customers. Ask yourself:

- *Who do you already know that could become a customer or a referral source for you?* Think neighbors, business contacts, former co-workers, church patrons, friends, hair stylists, dry cleaners, bank tellers, and more.
- *What are five businesses where your contacts or current customers could benefit from* ***their*** *services or product? How can you approach them and find out more about their story, with the goal of building relationships and*

mutually beneficial referral partnerships? Talk to them about why they work there and the deeper reasons behind their work. Ask them how to know when someone you meet is a good prospect for them!

- *How can you leverage newspapers, local magazines, and the internet to identify prospecting opportunities?*
- *What regular networking events can you join? Which ones will add value to you? How can you add value to those in attendance?*

When you make these efforts, some will greet you with a willingness to engage in a relationship, while others may think you insincere and just blow you off. To that I say, don't worry about people not liking you or taking offense. You are not going to be the answer for everyone, and that's okay. I find that it has always served me well to remember that at any time any president is disliked by at least forty-nine percent of the population, so you are in good company! What matters is that you truly believe that others need and want your help, and that you are capable of helping them—and that you know it's your moral obligation to do so.

In most sales relationships, you are going to have to show that you can create value for prospective customers at least five times before you are able to ask for the sale. Building relationships is only going to happen when you make a genuine attempt to learn about your prospective customer's needs, wants, goals, and desires. From there, attach those to your vision and work toward the sale by eliciting emotion from them. Quick and dirty sales will no longer sustain in today's world, where people can sniff out what is not authentic.

There are two simple rules that will make you successful. First, consistently find ways to add more value than anyone else in your industry. Second, connect with as many people as possible. The more people you impact, the more they will help impact you. Your goal should always be to cultivate enthusiasm as you set out to identify how your product or service can help others. Become the source or resource for meeting your customer's needs, exceed their expectations, and you will win.

Help Them See Themselves in You

Faced with the uphill battle of starting Providence Care with ten percent of the required capital, I needed to reach out to existing connections. I also knew that volunteering could provide a great route to broaden my community reach. To fulfill my personal desire to create value everywhere I went, I offered my time as a volunteer for Meals on Wheels. The opportunity came about after I read a newspaper article regarding a local chapter welcoming a new executive director to their team. I immediately felt a kinship with her story.

Making the fifteen-minute drive to her office, I walked in carrying three copies of the paper. After being greeted by the location gatekeeper, I asked, "Is Meta back in yet?" I asked, purposefully sounding like I already knew her. Her colleagues headed out back to let her know I was there and she came out to greet me. "Hi, Meta," I said. "I just had to come in and say congratulations for getting your picture in the paper. It's not every day that happens!" Before we had even begun, I had her blushing from my sincere admiration. The flattery wasn't fake, it was a feeling of here is someone like me, just starting off to help those in need and I sincerely appreciated it. I told her that I had brought her copies because her friends and family members might want their own. I then asked her about the worst route they had—the one nobody wanted to drive. That was the one I wanted to volunteer for. Why? Because it was perfectly aligned with Providence Care's willingness to go to the clients in places where other agencies did not want to go. It also didn't hurt that many of the Meals on Wheels customers were home-bound and potentially ideal clients for Providence Care.

As our conversation grew, Meta asked what I did for a living. I told her I had just started my own hospice care ministry. I shared my vision for serving the underserved. From the day I accepted the route that no one else wanted, until the day I sold the company a decade later, Providence consistently received three to six referrals a month from her homebound clients. Why? Because we created value *for them first*!

Help every prospective customer see themselves in your story—by painting vivid, emotion-based pictures and talking with others using empowering language. Your job is to help others fulfill whatever they wish to create. The quickest way to build a mutually beneficial relationship is through shared experiences. Become a great storyteller and identify your common ground, connecting the dots to bring them into your story. Invite them into your vision and show them how it can help meet their needs. Make yourself an integral part of their vision. Help them see themselves in you.

The moral of the story is that your sales efforts always need to be about meeting your customer's needs first. There is a psychology to sales. You must treat every prospective customer (or referral partner) like a relationship you sincerely care about. If you find you don't care about the relationship first, you don't deserve their trust. It always has to be about your target customers—what they need and their involvement with your product or service. It's the equivalent of taking a group photo and showing them where they are in your picture—and how you fit into theirs! Without this mutual fitting into each other's story there will never be the possibility of you serving their needs. In the overflow of the value you create for others, you will find your own needs being met in the process. It all comes down to asking several powerful questions and encouraging your team members to ask the same:

- *What are your target customer's goals and points of pain?*
- *What will you ask about their current condition (i.e., their needs, wants, and desires)?*
- *How can you attach their wants, needs and desires to yours, in a way that they are going to be met by buying from you?*
- *How can you position your message (and offer) so they see themselves in your story?*

Helping prospective customers feel truly understood involves grasping their motivations, comprehending their biases, and helping them meet their needs. Are they moving toward pleasure or away from pain? What you are ultimately doing with your sales relationships is building *trust*, or what I call "the consistent fulfillment of expectations." If a prospective customer doesn't trust you, they aren't going to buy. It's really no more or less complicated than that. To earn trust, you must constantly fulfill the expectations you have set. Do what you say you will do, when you say you will do it. Remember, however, this isn't about being perfect. You will miss the mark from time to time. Realize that hiccups or conflicts can become the back door to building trust, because they give you the opportunity to recover and exceed expectations moving forward.

Feelings Come First

At Providence Care, one of our sales reps was having trouble breaking through with a local hospital. They simply would not allow us to come in and educate them on our home-based, palliative care programs for their terminally ill patients. She felt confident we could help so many patients there, but the hospital gatekeeper was putting up what felt like an impenetrable brick wall. Our rep was growing more and more frustrated with the roadblock.

As I watched her beat her fists on the desk in my office, I asked her why she was so upset. She told me it was because one of her neighbors had just died on the way to this same hospital and he had never received the care he was entitled to. She felt like a failure knowing he had died in a state of chaos, not comfort. My advice to her was to follow her heart and just be honest and go back and tell the gatekeeper this!

The next day, she walked back into that hospital with the goal of securing an appointment to educate the hospital's discharge planners on how we can serve them. She entered the hospital gatekeeper's office and slammed down the newspaper she had in hand, passionately pointing out one specific obituary she had it opened to. "You see Mr. Johnson. He was my neighbor!" she said. "And he died on the way to this hospital. I know that if we would have had him on service, that would not have happened. There's your failure. This didn't have to happen this way, but because you denied him knowledge about what we can provide for our community, Mr. Johnson became a result of that." Following that conversation, not only did our rep get the appointment; the hospital signed on for our services. Passion comes first, sales come second. The rep had sold a very powerful feeling and made her story about the hospital and the fulfillment of their vision and reputation.

People don't buy products or services; they buy feelings and identity. Read that one again. You must get people emotionally involved before telling them how what you have to offer will meet their needs. Feelings need to come first and the justification for your offer second. We think we are rational people and that if we make a sound argument based on facts, people will be persuaded to buy from us. This is not the case, however. We talked about the need to be a great storyteller earlier, and here is where it comes into play again. When any of us experience a powerful story, we feel it in our body and it reverberates in our bones. It becomes part of us. Grab your prospective customers' hearts and their minds will follow.

To achieve feeling first, you have to understand what creates a feeling. We talked about using your language as leverage when establishing your culture. The same thing applies to every outreach to your customers. *The quality of your feelings = the quality of your thoughts = the quality of your words.* Feeling begins with the quality of your language. Use your words to inspire and create a feeling within others. It is within that feeling that your prospective customers will find their own justification for buying your product or service.

Your success will always be in direct proportion to your ability to communicate effectively. Ask specific questions and you will get specific responses; ask generically and you will get a generic response. In order to always strive to bring feeling to the forefront, use the following questions to attach emotion to every sales effort:

- *What language can you use to create relatability and persuade people?*
- *What vocabulary can you adapt that is positive, reinforcing, and emotion-based?*
- *How can you slow down and lower your voice to ensure your language is conveyed as caring and fostering a new relationship?*

When it comes to supporting your team members in the sales cycle, think back to the primary principle we described to keep you motivated: prepare, create, and celebrate. What did you and your team do to move the ball forward this week? What shared language is supporting the feeling behind the wins? Who did you help? Any efforts to build new relationships with prospective customers, referral partners, or your community should be celebrated, even when you are moving the ball forward just two inches! Success is contagious; sharing it will help rally your team together. Sales is not intended to be difficult, so simplify, simplify, simplify, because once you have mastered the sales cycle, the degree to which you can grow becomes limitless.

The Key Questions

You're Sold, Now Go Sell

- Understand the True Sales Cycle:
    - *What season are you currently in and how do you know? What season is your prospective customer in?*
    - *Who do you need to be in relationship with? How can you begin to establish those connections?*
    - *How can you leverage your current relationships? What committees or communities are you already part of?*
- Help Them See Themselves in You:
    - *What is your unique value proposition and how does that align with your prospective customer's needs, wants, and desires?*
    - *What will be the key language you will use in your sales conversations?*
- Feelings Come First:
    - *What is your prospective customer feeling after your conversation? Have you left them feeling reassured, secure, protected, and prepared?*
    - *Have your interactions with prospective customers helped to build trust and respect?*

Take Action

1. **Identify twenty potential prospects:** Who could benefit from your product or service? Begin with a clear vision of how you plan to communicate the reasons behind what you do, then reach out and seek to learn about your customers. Aim to secure at least four conversations or appointments, depending on the scope of the product or service you are selling. Have as your goal securing a sale with at least one of the twenty prospects.
2. **Look for unique prospecting opportunities and create power challenges:** Perhaps write a thank you note on your business card and hand it to a stranger standing in a line with you at a grocery store, the bank, etc. Tell them you are thanking them in advance for thinking of you in the future! As a power challenge, have your team members approach five businesses during lunch. Tell them they need to walk in, find out who the manager or owner is, and discover why they started their business and who would be a perfect referral for them—someone you could send their way. If they can't do that, how can they sell your product or service? They can't.
3. **Create an environment where forward progress is ever-present:** Continuously celebrate the small wins and keep the fire of momentum stoked by reminding your team members where you have come from and

> where you are going. That boost of emotion creates motion, which will further fuel sales momentum and forward progress.

You must love your vision, but you must also love how your vision enhances your clients' lives even more. Passion comes first and profits come last. When you believe in what you are doing and are in the pursuit of creating value for others, the "scoreboard" (namely the profits) will take care of itself. Sales is not about bothering others to get them to buy something they don't need; it's about *seeing their needs and helping meet them.* Be the enterprise that continuously sets out to help others have a better day tomorrow. Simplify, be in season, and be strategic. Above all, believe in what you do and focus on the feeling associated with what you are selling. Confidence in sales is a direct result of an unshakeable, burning belief that the lives of others will be made better by becoming a part of your product or service. If you don't believe that, neither will your prospective customers!

RISE ABOVE THE STORMS AND DOLDRUMS

The load never gets lighter;
you just get stronger.

Your ability to hold the weight increases in proportion to the character you build.

MILESTONE 7: ELEVATE CHARACTER AND COMMITMENT

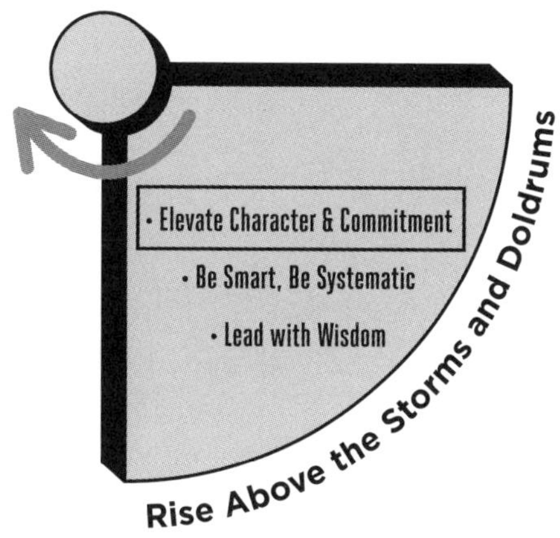

ELEVATE CHARACTER AND COMMITMENT

Let me tell you a story. Once upon a time, there was a sailor who set out on a fantastic voyage. Although the exact location of his destination lay hidden far beyond the clouds, his focus and excitement about arriving were clear. The forecast was predicting blue skies and calm seas. Having checked his vessel from stem to stern—his compass set and the shrouds made ready to hold their heel—he lifted his fingers to the wind. All checks were go, as the sails filled and the conch shell blew the blessing of his departure. He could feel passion and excitement brewing within him at the thought of reaching the shores of his destination.

For the first leg of his journey, the ocean was warm and inviting, as he rode out radiant sunrises and navigated nights of incredible stargazing. As the waves rolled in, he was rounding each waypoint without incident. It had all been going so smoothly, until he awoke one morning to red skies—a harbinger of a storm on the rise. The warning had not lied, as the winds suddenly began to shift and the seas churned beneath him. It all felt like a broken promise, casting aside the tranquility he had known from his initial days at sea. In his gut, he felt exhilaration now intermixed with a new feeling. Doubt had risen to the surface, making the sailor question whether he had what it would take to navigate the chaos and reach his destination. Could he lean on his knowledge, experience, and talent to ready the tack and anticipate the jibes coming his way?

Even in the midst of his inability to control the tempest, the sailor found it in himself to hold strong to the belief that he had what it took to journey onward. Then, just as he was harnessed into his new position of unsettled seas, from seemingly out of nowhere came a deafening silence and an uncanny calm. The storm had suddenly passed, taking with it all of his momentum. His mast and sails lay hanging lifeless, the ship's flags went still, and there was no movement or sound. As the wind fell quiet, a new fear took a hold of him. Had he seen the end of his forward progress and of the dream of reaching his destination? It felt as though his driving force had died and the days of progress under the crisp, blue skies and sun were a distant memory. The indifferent sea left him questioning how he was going to recover and press forward. What was he to do when he felt powerless to overcome the silence and the stillness?

Day after day, day after day,
We stuck, nor breath nor motion;
As idle as a painted ship
Upon a painted ocean.

—"The Rime of the Ancient Mariner"
by Samuel Taylor Coleridge, 1798

In this third phase of your journey, shaping your vision for your team or enterprise, you are faced with the momentous task of rising above the storms and doldrums—the expected and unexpected challenges that will come your way. At this point, having launched your vision into action by powering the development of your initial team and sales efforts, you have hopefully gained some nice momentum. It has likely felt as though you are steadily making gains every day—new team members, new agreements, new relationships. People are buying into your idea that things are feeling well, much like the calm waters and blue skies the sailor knew for his first few days at sea. All of this has hopefully helped you come into your own with a new sense of identity and assurance, as you step deeper into clarity about what your offer is—and what it is not—and the real impact it can have. This building of confidence, along with a steady rise of your motivation, has brought a renewed sense of hope and purpose that what you have long envisioned for your enterprise will indeed work out.

However, you are also fully aware that you are seated squarely in middle of the honeymoon phase—filled with passion, hopefulness, vision, giving, and receiving. You also know that no honeymoon phase lasts forever.

There is no denying that one of life's golden rules is that where there has been success, there will always come a test—one designed to see if you truly believe in what you are striving for. Just as you have discovered a new stride in your step, the road ahead is inevitably going to bring forth new problems, in the form of storms and doldrums. Some you won't anticipate, while others will come with a rush. A promising big account doesn't come through or there is stagnation in your sales momentum. It may also come in the form of a tax audit or policy you didn't see coming, or shifting industry regulations. It may be a team member who left with your intellectual property, or a wrongful termination lawsuit you know to be unfounded.

Rubber, let me introduce you to the road! Things are now going to grow tougher in a very real, raw way. You'll find yourself having to reconcile how your role and vision fit with reality. You begin to notice the differences between what you once believed about how incremental success should look versus how it looks when you factor in the unexpected. This can easily fuel a feeling that your motivation is waning and raise the question, *is this all there is?* After sailing the waves of initial growth, new challenges can feel as though they have taken some of the wind out of your sails. There may be fear that problems can halt your progress. Worse yet, they may be your ruin. This can be the point where it feels easier to consider potential exit ramps and asking yourself whether it would be easier to end the struggle than to persevere. But this chapter is about averting these pitfalls and building your character and commitment in the process. These two factors are the magic sauce to help you find your way through times of struggle.

Pain will come; that's okay. In hard times, my grandfather used to remind me that the Bible repeatedly states, "and it came to pass." He would add, "Remember, it didn't come to stay."

After having had some success, now you're focused on coming out stronger on the other side. Going forward, simply being good is not going to be good enough. What you do amid the storms and doldrums will dictate the sustainability of your success. If you were that sailor in the boat, would you break out the satellite phone and call for help, or would you try to work your way out of the problem yourself? The answer will tell you what you need to know about your current level of character and commitment—and how much room you have to grow in order to press forward. How you proceed and who you need to become is about building character, applying commitment, and learning how to anticipate and prepare for what is coming.

Things are inevitably going to become harder after your initial rise in momentum, and you never want to fall victim to the unexpected. This is your chance to assess where you are and regain any lost mojo—two elements you want to practice daily with your team. It's time to show your unflappable commitment and reapply your values as actionable plans that will help you navigate in times of challenge. That's what the seventh milestone is all about.

Know How to Grow Character

You are actively growing character when everything seems to hurt, and yet, you are still alive. Four years into starting Providence Care, we had opened our third location and were growing by twenty to thirty percent year-over-year. We were not only disrupting failure; we were disrupting healthcare as an industry, which was a very good thing. Unsolicited referrals and employment applications were rolling in weekly, with top talent seeking us out. The energy bubbling from below the surface was exciting and everyone on the team was having fun. Behind the scenes, my perspective was different. I worried we didn't have the systems and processes in place to sustain growth at such a level.

Sure enough, not long after, we discovered that our growth had led to the compounding of a building storm we were unaware of—one that stopped us in our tracks. Our rapid expansion had flagged a Medicare audit. After four years of thinking we were classified under one branch of the program, and were following all of its rules, a recent change revealed that things had shifted and that we had not adapted. We had been calculating the value of Medicare services incorrectly, because our patients were outliving their benefits and the additional services we had provided were not covered. The miscalculation had us owing $1.8 million back to Medicare for the previous three years.

Before that, regular meetings with our CFO left me reassured that everything was fine. While a buzz of eager energy could be felt everywhere else, her office always seemed far too quiet. Either she was Wonder Woman and deserved a huge raise for excellence, or things were being missed and were about to implode. My answer became clear one Monday morning after the Medicare audit results were delivered. I arrived at the office to discover that she had moved everything out and left a note that read, "I did the best I could and I quit!" The pin had been pulled on the grenade as she walked away, and those of us on the team were left to triage the crisis and figure out how we would recover.

Dr. Romin and I talked it out as we tried to calm our nerves by smoking cigars on my boat dock. Feeling as though the end may be near and there was no way out of this doldrum, we reminisced about all that we had created thus far and the lives that had been changed for the better. Romin later told me that he was ready to head back to work for the hospital and was thankful for the ride. However, I had no fall-back plan and there was no way I was going so quietly without a fight. I knew that our heart was in the right place, even if we did the wrong thing. That had to be good for something. I refused to let Providence Care falter and took ownership for our ignorance with the Medicare calculations, blaming nothing on anyone else. Even though my ex-CFO was charged with proper reimbursement calculations, it was ultimately my responsibility and mine alone. What happened was due to my ignorance and oversight, and I was going to fix it.

Thinking to the past, I began by looking at what I had done during the most challenging times in my life: my divorce and being fired from Hallmark. How did those challenges serve me and what had they allowed me to become? How had I managed to disrupt failure? Could I do the same when faced with this enormous feat? I would ask myself these questions until the answers came.

Reviewing the tools and resources at our disposal, I spearheaded efforts to create what was now required to chart our course forward. I also worked to determine who was best suited to help lead us through this unexpected hit. For the next year, I was laser-focused, determined to lead the team to find a way through the unexpected storm. Medicare knew we had miscalculated, and we were doing everything possible to find a way to pay the money back. To save on costs, I stopped paying myself and Romin a salary and benefits. I sold everything I could to raise money to keep the mission afloat. I even moved my family into a home half the size of the one we were living in at the time. Any profit was immediately put back into the company. I shut down an underperforming office, consolidated resources, released unneeded employees and discharged patients to comply with our new understanding of Medicare guidelines. It wasn't easy, but I knew we had to get small in order to grow bigger. Romin infused the company with cash where he was able to and the two of us shouldered as much of the brunt as possible, as we went back to the beginning and rebuilt. Despite our youthful ambitions and wanting to say *yes* to everyone, we were facing the inevitable dance between cost and care. Fixing the immediacy of the current doldrum had shifted our trajectory. While we were not going to change our vision (our destination), we had to pull out our map and chart a new direction to get there.

My hope for you is that you'll be prepared and aware at this stage of your journey. To evolve and continue growing (and disrupting failure), you will need to *step into every situation with a willingness to solve problems.* This is the phase driving you from motivation (where you have been) to commitment (where you need to be now). It is being conscious about how you respond to the small hiccups as well as the big storms, knowing that each misstep can build up to a giant sinkhole over time. Character is not given. It's developed through your ability to endure pain, form wisdom, and become more adept at using that wise perspective to find joy in your circumstance. It is developed and continually refined as you face the decision of whether to stay or go—to step into the storm or take the exit ramp. The price of worthy or honorable leadership will most often be paid through pain, as character is built *within challenge.*

You may forget the details of an experience, even the most challenging one, but neither you nor anyone else will forget *who you are during that experience.* Someone is always watching you—your team, your customers, or both. You need to build the character required to define yourself as a consistent, committed person. You need to be someone who continues to believe in the vision you initially rallied others around and who stays true to who you are—your values. There is no playing the victim here; you must be responsible and accountable. You are the foundation of what you have built. You can always delegate tasks to others, but you can never abandon your responsibility to the outcome. Understand that challenges present themselves to make you better. The person you were when you began this vision is not who you are going to be when you arrive! When you remain resolute and do not falter, your capacity will grow and so will your ability to hold the weight.

The deeper your commitment, the longer you will be able to sustain the pain. Each time you weather the storm and rise to the occasion, the stronger you will become. Overcoming challenges builds confidence, and a rise in character will give you the confidence to walk bravely into the bigger storms. That willingness to run into what is coming will increase the rate at which you achieve a solution. It all begins by testing your character to reveal whether your values and priorities continue to align with who you say you are. Doing so will reveal whether you have what it takes to navigate the stormy seas. Here are questions to constantly be asking yourself:

- *Are your current actions a true statement of who you are?*
- *Could you publish what you have done on the front page of the* New York Times *and be proud of it?*
- *How are your current storms and doldrums serving you by allowing you to further develop your character? How can you embrace this opportunity for growth?*

Learn to make hard decisions with integrity; they will be where true character is made and revealed. The choices you face during the hard times will be a catalyst for growth—an opportunity for developing the character needed to become the kind of leader who merits reaching the ultimate destination. Watch your words. If you aren't able to put your words in print and be proud of them, then don't speak them! If you aren't willing to have a prosecuting attorney read an email or statement back to you and feel as though you can defend it, then don't say it! There is no right way to do the wrong thing, and your character will be defined by these moments. If you dance outside of your values, out of the need for an urgent response, you may find your way back to momentary success, but you will not see it sustain for the long term.

You Need the Storms. Welcome Them.

I have always been fascinated by the excitement countless people feel about playing the lottery, and what they believe it could hold for potentially making their every dream a reality. To me, playing the lottery is like standing outside under sunny skies and hoping lightning will strike. That said, there is also something intriguing about reading the story of that one-in-a-million winner who becomes a multimillionaire overnight. It gives a certain hope to the slim possibility of any of us becoming a winner.

The allure of millions may seem enticing, though it begs the bigger question of whether that is what we truly want. In reality, on the flip side of this idealistic picture, an estimated thirty to seventy percent of lottery winners are likely to go bankrupt within three to five years of winning![2] How is it that a windfall of cash can so quickly result in bankruptcy? From my point of view, it all comes back to the defining character developed within. When you immediately inherit a destination without its challenges, there is no journey to building character and no wise perspective is developed. Because commitment is weak and there isn't adequate wisdom and experience, poor decisions are made. This is where most leaders falter and why even though we hate it, we need the desert before we can inherit the promised land. The deserts are where character is built. It is not enough to create something quickly; you must sustain it. Sustaining success requires much more than mere luck. Much like the quick rise of Providence Care's growth over its first three years, we had to reassess, pivot, and have our character tested in order to grow in a sustainable way.

Sustainability and true impact necessitate consistency and discipline—that which can only be built during the challenges of the journey. Anyone can hit a great shot on the golf course once, but the difference between a PGA pro and an everyday golfer lies in the ability to *sustain* great hits. Consistency is your ability to recreate a desired result at will. It is possible only through endless daily dedication to what right looks like. That's how you form commitment. When you think of this in relation to your day-to-day leadership, it means upholding your dedication to the principles, standards, and values at the foundation of your team or enterprise—doing what you need to do, even when you don't feel like doing it! As storms and doldrums arise, your commitment, like your character, will be challenged. The greater your commitment to pursuing your vision ethically and consistently, the longer you will persevere. The longer you persevere, the greater your character will become. The greater your character, the more wisdom you will gain. You can only gain wisdom by doing things over and over again! From that point, the greater your wisdom grows, the better your discernments and decisions will be.

It is worth repeating: when you find yourself or your team struggling with storms and doldrums, the answers you need may be found by asking a different question, or by asking the same question differently! Your questions will be the rudder that helps you stay on course. Here are some powerful, commitment-oriented points to always be asking yourself when challenges arise:

- *What are the top three changes causing the current problem?*
- *What untapped resources do you currently have that can be redirected to address these changes?*
- *What relationship do you have or need to have that can assist you?*
- *What deficit do you have and how can you mitigate that?*

Your ultimate value doesn't just lie in your being great; it lies in you continuously helping those around you become better! After taking a studied look in the mirror, and making strides to develop your own character and commitment, it is time to create the environment and culture that allow your team members to do the same.

There is great value in bringing certainty to an uncertain future. That's what your job is. A big part of it comes back to the collective thoughts held by your team. We talked about the importance of language earlier, and here it is again. During times of change, internalize and question the sentiments below and adapt them to your own culture. They can serve as some of the most powerful insights for every team member during good times and trying times, in order to foster collective character and commitment:

- *Things are going to get uncomfortable at times and that's okay.*
- *We are going to mess up and that is to be expected.*
- *Some will have their eyes opened, and some will have them closed … though the opportunity for growth remains the same for all.*
- *We all deal with stress differently. Some of us will feel excitement or exhilaration in the thick of the storm. It is up to us to step forward and share that sentiment with others.*
- *Some will feel confused and afraid.*
- *We will always choose to work as one, pulling together to work through and rise above the storms and doldrums.*
- *We will remain prepared and put safety first, in order to ensure we are successful.*
- *It came to pass. It didn't come to stay!*

Everything, including character and commitment, is part of the foundation; and you are the foundation. As the leader of your team, you must carry the load and strive to help everyone constantly get better—and grow more prepared for the storms and doldrums. When you look back at all that you've been able to do, you can recognize there is an incredible structure forming from what you have already created. Look closely and you will likely see that you have within you all you need to navigate tumultuous seas. Show your team what you did to develop character and commitment, and let them see the outcomes that were realized. Explain the decisions that directly affect them, and why you made them. Show them the challenges, the reasons, and the repercussions. Unless there are legal or ethical reasons not to, good leaders tell their teams everything there is to know so that team members can take co-ownership of the experience. This will help reduce fear and uncertainty. Building character and commitment is never going to be a one-and-done process; it must become something that you live on a daily basis.

Expect and Prepare

At the beginning of the chapter, we recounted the tale of a sailor, but there is more to the story. While he remained optimistic in hoping for the best and was well prepared for his journey, he also knew he needed to prepare for the worst. Before ever boarding his ship, he had filed a float plan that included check-in times with those who could support him if he got off-track or caught in a storm. He had created a pool of shared knowledge he could tap into from those who had made the journey before. In addition to putting in place the supports for his original plan, he had also plotted an alternative course to his destination, in the case the original route proved impassable. He had gathered adequate food supplies, as well as provisioning for fifty percent more than what he thought he would need. He had a working life boat, safety equipment, and a ditch bag on board that included all of his necessities.

Preparation is power, as you understand and anticipate the person you need to become to get to the other side. Tomorrow is never going to be like today. Proactively building character and commitment is about finding a friend in the storms. This happens by learning how to expect and prepare for them. Get better sooner rather than later. Read, study, train, and prepare. Things will only get better when you do! Being stuck in concrete will never stimulate your personal growth, nor that of your team. Immobility is never an option when you are being called to rise to the occasion.

Many times, warning signs don't precede the storms and doldrums. Sometimes they are a waypoint on the track to who you can become as a leader in order to grow your business. It all comes back to the importance of movement. As you face new problems, your challenge will lie in maintaining your forward motion. Without movement, it can quickly begin to feel as though your motivation is gone and the doldrums have won. Your success will be determined by the speed at which you become who you are intended to be. It matters how you step into the arena! Before we get into the intricacies of how to solve problems, this work is about dedicating yourself to a mindset and the preparatory work that must precede your problem-solving actions. Here are some powerful concepts you can program into your mind—and into the minds of your team members:

- *Expect the storms and doldrums; they are there to grow you, not destroy you.*
- *Apply purpose to the pain. It will still be hard, but you'll know on the other side of pain will come a better version of you!*
- *Know that the storms and doldrums "came to pass," not to stay.*

- *Storms love to isolate, so stay connected. Counter the nature of the storm to isolate you by being around others who offer sage advice and ongoing motivation.*
- *Pick your pain every day. Remember the pain of going back to where you were before you ignited your vision into this reality. Keep that written on your heart.*
- *Reevaluate your systems. What works in one season or for a past problem won't necessarily work for the current one.*
- *Keep moving and don't change your destination. Focus on your speed over your direction, while remaining pointed toward your vision. Progress will not come if you're not moving!*

When you can anticipate what is coming to a certain degree, it will free you from worry. Building a strong mentality within your team means trusting that collectively you have what it takes to navigate the rough or stagnant seas.

The Key Questions

The Rise of Character and Commitment

- Know How to Grow Character:
    - *When you look at your responses to storms and doldrums, are you currently as good as you need to be (or as your team believes you to be)?*

- *Who are you at the core and are you showing all of yourself to your team, customers, and stakeholders? Has this remained consistent through each storm or doldrum you face?*
- You Need the Storms. Welcome Them:
  - *Look at your past week, month, and year and the challenges you have faced. Have you remained consistent in your response and committed to your values and vision?*
  - *How can you show your team the opportunity for growth being presented by current storms and doldrums?*
- Expect and Prepare:
  - *How can a storm you are facing serve you? How does it present an opportunity to do what you weren't previously able to do?*
  - *What standard will you set for your team's approach to storms and doldrums?*

Take Action

1. **Evaluate your willingness to solve problems, big and small:** Adopt a third-person perspective to yourself and rank your response to the latest challenges you have faced. Did you respond in alignment with your values? Did your character remain true, or is there

room for growth? What needs to change to help you rise to the occasion of the next doldrum?

2. **Foster commitment by creating a power start to every team meeting:** You can elicit teamwork, clarity, and strength by beginning every meeting with an intention statement. For instance, *the outcome I hope we can get to is [__________], the purpose of this action is [_________],* or *our intention here is to [__________].* Make this a regular practice.
3. **Take note of the cycles that others in your industry have gone through:** A good leader must be a great observer—of people, of the challenges facing your industry, and of other organizations. You are never going to be the exception to the rules, nor are you going to escape without scars, so it's best to strive to anticipate and prepare for what is coming!

Every enterprise has their stories of highs and lows—tales filled with struggles, triumphs, setbacks, courage, fear, and tears. They are what has made and will make your enterprise what it is. In their highest capacity, your storms and doldrums serve as the medium and opportunity for you to develop character and hone your long-term commitment. This point in the process presents an opportunity to work on your own personal development and teach what you have learned to your team. Character and commitment will distinguish your enterprise as either a short-lived success or a long-term legacy. This is your opportunity to fortify and reinforce everything you have said you believe in and to uphold it. Master the character- and commitment-building principles in this chapter and you will have created something that gives you a firm grasp of the science of success. You get to decide if you will be a one-hit wonder or if you have what it takes to sustain and achieve a fulfilled vision.

There are only two functions in business: fixing problems or seizing opportunities under the umbrella of building relationships.

MILESTONE 8: BE SMART, BE SYSTEMATIC

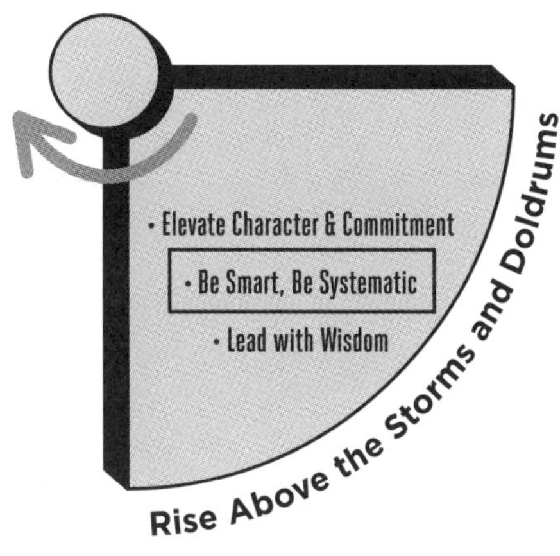

BE SMART, BE SYSTEMATIC

Whether we realize it or not, we all have rituals and daily habits. In order to run a household, raise a family, or simply head off to work, we all use routines. Some wake up, brush their teeth, and hit the gym long before most have even started their day. For others, it is totally different. Their mornings may involve reaching for that first cigarette and cup of coffee, that's needed to jumpstart their day.

Rituals are the choices and actions we take every day in the broader context of our lives. However, they are not simply something that we do in the privacy of our homes! Our habits are the catalysts to what we become and what others see us becoming—from our physical health to our ability to show up where we are needed. Habits differ in their results. A lifestyle of countless cigarettes and a poor diet are certainly not going to make you as healthy as someone with a ritual of rising early to hit the gym and eating healthy foods. Your routine becomes your reality! The daily rituals, systems, and habits you undertake have a direct impact on the quality of your life and the lives of everyone in your orbit. Change your system—your daily way of life—and you change your outcome!

Smart problem solvers have a reproducible process that leads to a high-quality, predictable experience—one that dictates how you operate and execute your customer interactions. Your eighth milestone is all about being smart and systematic. This chapter will show you how to build the systems for questioning, categorizing, and hacking problems that inevitably creep into your enterprise.

Now that you've built a solid foundation for your vision and launched it effectively, it is now time to make everything run like clockwork! You have either reached, or are nearing the point where you have shaped something beyond what you can manage alone. It's time to fire yourself and become the least important person in the room.

You are going to do this by creating the systems for success. You want to build an enterprise that can run independently and outlive you. This is about becoming intentional and systematic with every decision, as you learn to lean on the tools, tricks, and tactics you have built. That way, you can get back to spending your days focusing on seizing new opportunities—working *on* the business rather than *in* the business. You can feel confident that your team members are all working off the same page, following the proven systems you have established.

It's time to spearhead the processes that will shape a new way of thinking. That's because what got you here, to this point, will no longer work in reaching the next level of the vision! Heart, passion, and even a strength of character will not be enough to realize success from here on. As you continue to expand, unfamiliar problems big and small will increasingly find their way in, and you need to be in the driver's seat. You need systems that will lead to predictable results for you and your team, in order for you to create something even bigger and better than you thought it could be.

Growth in life and in business will always be about managing well. What you mismanage will be taken from you. It's just that simple. Fail to properly manage your personal relationships and they will fall apart. Fail to manage your health, ignoring exercise and proper eating, and you are going to get sick. Fail to manage problems within your business and they will overtake your momentum and sink your ship. Disrupting these failures happens when you act smart, having proactively set up systems to anticipate and solve problems coming your way. Be clear on the fact that business and leadership only have two functions: solving problems and seizing opportunities. Anything else is background noise and distraction. Influence and success will expand or contract based on your problem-solving and decision-making ability. If you aren't great at either of these, the culture and foundation will crack and what you have created will not stand long enough for your vision to materialize into its full potential.

Know When a Problem Is Actually a Decision

At the same time Providence Care was facing the monumental task of paying back almost $2 million to Medicare, another storm came our way. Earlier that same year, we had purchased a run-down Howard Johnson hotel with the vision of converting it into an assisted-living community for low-income families. As with any big decision, I had known it would take time, investment, and patience to see things pay off. We had begun by investing a quarter-million dollars for the architects and floor plans that would bring our community to life. In the midst of planning, the area's flood zone mapping suddenly and unexpectedly changed. To make the space a reality, we were now going to have to put in retention walls, elevate the first-floor rooms and common areas, redesign the remaining space, and recalculate our revenue to align with a loss of available patient rooms—all at a cost of millions of dollars. The potential profitability of this new venture was quickly disappearing.

With any expensive decision, you must have a plan in case the worst happens. Before purchasing the hotel, I had questioned the possible outcomes of a worst-case scenario. Could I liquidate the hotel and protect our downside if needed? When the conditions that caused us to purchase the hotel changed, we had to execute on those worst-case plans and sell it quickly, before it cost us even more. This was an example of my pre-planned "ditch bag." It was a choice made at a time when most of our cash flow was going toward repaying Medicare.

Hiring my realtor sister to get it done, we went back to the original brokers to find out who their secondary offers had been. Perhaps one of those eager buyers would want a second shot at a winning bid for the hotel? Our pitch to a potential buyer was that they would get the space they wanted, but also have the new surveys and flood zone plans as a bonus. By adding value, creating a scenario that was about them, and making it easy for another potential buyer to say *yes*, we were able to quickly liquidate and resume our plans of consolidating and cutting costs in order to repay Medicare.

Was what I faced a problem or a decision—or both? Most leaders have no idea. That is where your efforts at being smart and systematic must begin! Before diving into diagnosing and solving problems, the first critical step is to *know whether you are dealing with a problem or a decision.* Many leaders perceive problems and decisions as interchangeable or synonymous, when in actuality, they are very different. The distinction is simple to understand and here is what distinguishes the two:

Problems:

- **What is it:** You are dealing with a problem when whatever used to happen a certain way met or exceeded expectations (i.e., was working) but no longer does. For example, a stellar employee, one you had always been able to count on, is no longer doing their job well.
- **Diagnosis:** Problems are more easily identified and diagnosed than decisions, because you have already done the work to identify what right looks like. Now, you should be able to clearly see what is not right. Identifying problems can be less time-consuming because the questions asked to determine what went wrong are more direct. You don't have to go through trial and error, as you would when braving the new territory of a decision.
- **Cause:** To determine the source of a problem (what caused a negative change where there once was success), begin by asking questions: *What is different? Why does it no longer work or meet expectations?* (Bear in mind that sometimes it is your expectations that have changed, so maybe the problem is you!)

Somewhere in these questions, you will begin to discover what has changed.

- **Execution:** The time commitment for solving a problem will be directly correlated to the size of the problem and the systems you have in place.

Decisions:

- **What is it:** You are dealing with a decision when something has *never* worked in the past and is still not working. It has never produced acceptable results. For example, you hired an employee to perform a job and that person has never been able to do the work, even after training, coaching, or motivating them. Decisions can also be required where a new program has never gotten off the ground, or a new policy has led to the same recurring, unintended consequences.
- **Diagnosis:** The answer as to what right looks like isn't always going to be clear up front. That's because you haven't been down this road before! That is why decisions tend to require a lot more commitment, and a lot more time and testing, and finally, a lot more patience.
- **Cause:** Whenever you are faced with making a decision, the first question to ask would be: *Is this an exception or a rule?* This is an absolutely essential question, since decisions should only be made to address the exceptions to the rules, not the rules themselves. A well-planned

enterprise should already have policies in place to address rules.

- **Execution:** The process of decision-making is one that develops over weeks, months, or even years. It must be managed, tried, and controlled. This is a stark contrast to the conventional view that a lone decision-maker should make choices in solitude.

You cannot properly address a problem or a decision without knowing which one you are dealing with! You will forever be forcing a round peg into a square hole. When you are able to identify problems versus decisions, you will save time, energy, and resources, because you will have clarity on what you are pursuing and how to pursue it.

Diagnose the Problem

Effectively diagnosing a problem is much like having a favorite old analog watch that has stopped working. It had been running perfectly, keeping you on track, but lately you noticed it has been getting a little sluggish. At first, it was slipping one second at a time, but eventually, it was off by a few hours. Whether you are a watch maker or an owner, your need to fix the watch would likely begin with a close examination of every gear and spring. Focusing on the small pieces, you would perform a careful walk-through of each system, attempting to isolate the malfunction. You'd know this takes patience and time, but you are willing to do the work. You'd like it done right the first time and without damage to other parts, so before making any attempts to fix it, you also want to be sure to identify the exact cause of the problem.

Before proposing a solution, you must be able to properly define the full scope of your problem. Misdiagnose a problem and you will be left wondering why the attempted solution isn't working! Get the diagnosis right and your problem-solving efforts will prove to be effective and efficient. Problem solving is a process built by asking the right questions and examining what is present, as well as what may be missing:

1. The first question of problem diagnosis, as we covered in the last section, will always be ***is this a problem or a decision?*** When you have determined it is a decision, do not go beyond the next step. Instead, begin the lengthy process of planning, testing, undertaking, and studying the effects of your new decision.
2. Your second question will be ***is this the exception or the rule?*** You don't want to waste too much time on something that is an exception! But if you start to see a trending issue, what used to be an exception has become a rule—and it's time to take problem-solving action! Begin by questioning whether you have a policy that addresses it. (Chances are you do when it's the rule!) If not, has a change in your environment necessitated a new policy? What do your core values say about this? Use them as your guidepost when you don't yet have a policy.
3. The third question then must be ***is this a temporary or permanent problem?***

- **Temporary problems** are those that will not reoccur. They only require temporary solutions, such as a quick resolution to a lack of cash flow. You don't need to solve a temporary problem with a permanent solution, until it is recurring (i.e., until it becomes a permanent problem).
- **Permanent problems** are those you are going to be dealing with for the foreseeable future, such as a new tax rate, new competition, or laws that must be complied with—These require well-thought-out, permanent solutions and policies in place. You also need to build the team and processes to manage them.

4. Finally, you need to properly investigate ***what type of problem you are facing***. There are three potential avenues:
    - **People problems** involve anyone you have a relationship with—a sales rep who used to meet their quota and now doesn't; an employee who always used to show up on time and is now always late; a mentor who used to help you so much, but no longer does.
    - **Product problems** occur when your products serve a need that no longer exists, like attempting to sell a Walkman to the general public in the digital age. A change in regulations or technology may have made the product obsolete. Product problems can also involve supply chain issues, like being unable to source the components to make it.

- **Process problems** can occur when new variants are introduced in your environment, causing an existing process to no longer work. They can happen even when you think you have good processes in place. The result is having to look at the side effects and downsides of your processes, as well as question why something is no longer working.

Solving problems is an unavoidable part of any enterprise, but there are many ways to ensure you approach the doldrums that creep up in a timely and effective manner. Identifying the precise problem or decision is more than half the battle; proper diagnoses help make problems feel more controlled and well-managed. They also mitigate the volume of surprises waiting to pop out from within each problem. By knowing precisely what you are facing, you reduce external noise and create space to focus on effectively fixing the issue.

Identify the Cause and Solve the Problem

Imagine you have spent the last three nights suffering from tremendous back pain. After reaching your breaking point, enduring more discomfort than you can tolerate, you make a doctor's appointment. The first question they ask is, "What is the problem that you have?" You tell them about suffering with back pain for the past three days. What happens if the physician immediately prescribes a specific medication, telling you to go home and take it, without ever having examined you or asking any investigative questions? There was no inquiry made into your pain history, previous injuries, other symptoms, lifestyle, or potential triggers. There were also no questions about how long the pain has persisted or how it originated. The physician's diagnosis was given with your simple report of back pain, taken at face value. The prescribed medication may not alleviate the pain and may lead to more serious long-term effects. If this was your experience, how much confidence would you have in the physician, the process they followed, or the remedy they prescribed?

When it comes to problem solving, most people use biases, quick judgments, and emotions based on limited knowledge or questioning. We all have our biases and life experiences as to what works and what doesn't. This can derail what resolving a problem truly requires. In leadership, there is often a tendency to do the exact same thing as the physician. It feels easier to take things at face value when an employee walks into our office with a problem. We listen just enough to jump to a predetermined conclusion and offer a quick solution. Without having an unbiased, systemic approach to investigating problems, there is a high likelihood that you will offer the wrong solution—one that does not address the root cause.

You need a concrete plan to identify the cause of your problems and solve them effectively. Here is my proven problem-solving system you can hardwire within your team, that will help alleviate the burden and decrease the unwanted side effects of a decision. The process involves addressing each of the following:

1. **Clearly define the problem and its root cause:** A problem-solving system is only going to work when you address the root cause and not the symptoms. *Most will try to solve a problem where it was found, not where it started.* To effectively resolve a problem,

you have to *go back to the root of where the problem began*! If you run out of gas at mile marker ten, where can you fix the problem? At mile marker five, where the gas station is! You have got to go back.

2. **Gather all relevant information surrounding the problem:** What has changed? What is different now versus when you set expectations which are no longer being met? Are you dealing with a mountain or a molehill? What is the delta between where you are and where you want to be? Are you ten percent towards the solution or ninety percent? These inquiries will help you define the scope of the problem and change the dynamic of the conversation. Make sure you quantify and put numbers to where things stand.
3. **Make a rational judgment and establish a goal:** Once you have identified the discrepancy between where things are and where they used to be, you can build a game plan to get things back on track. However, you don't just want to get back to breaking even; you want to add so much value that you come out better than before and the problem doesn't re-emerge. We have already discussed the need to ask *what right looks like*; this step focuses on reaching your next level by asking *what better looks like*!
4. **Gain or regain commitment:** Are there any reasons why your proposed solution will not work? Are there any potential roadblocks? Are there team members

who will require further support to build buy-in? I like to call this part of the process "putting people on HIPP (highly individualized protection plans)." This is about making a high-touch effort to sell your solution, reset expectations, and nurture your team to be a part of the change. Negotiate as required to gain or regain trust in the process.

The tool I created to achieve all of the above is what I call the Problem Pane.

The Problem Pane

Don't Know	Don't Have the Ability
Inform - Show, instruct, explain expectations. **Reset expectations -** Solicit feedback if not clearly defined or accepted. Adjust as needed. **(Re)educate -** Inquire why they didn't know and teach to alleviate.	**Determine if fit for duty -** Test (in safe, controlled environment) to see if expectations can be met. **Coach them -** Develop a plan for strengthening weaknesses. **Mentor them -** Create a strategy. Pair with a mentor who can teach hands on.
Don't Have the Tools	**Don't Care (Enough)**
Invest in equipment - What failed? What might you need? **Create new systems -** Did a system falter, or was it not properly used? **Offer alternative ways -** Identify other current resources to procure results.	**Motivate -** Determine current driving factors. Attempt to engage. **Accept their resignation / terminate -** Release so they may pursue a better fit elsewhere.

In my years of consulting and leading businesses, it became clear to me that the cause of behavioral or task-oriented problems originates from one of four categories:

1. an employee didn't know what needed to be done, or
2. they didn't have the ability, or
3. they didn't have the tools, or
4. they didn't care enough to meet the expectation.

Begin with identifying the real reason why expectations are no longer being met. Once you know whether you are dealing with a people, process, or product problem, you need to stay within the boundaries of these criteria when looking for a solution. When you identify which of these four quadrants your problem fits, you work through the solutions offered. This tool helps focus on both temporary and permanent problems in a methodical, non-biased, and non-threatening way. It gives you a platform for consistency across all departments and puts your entire enterprise on the same page, as you solve problems *together*—not in a *you versus them* scenario.

As an example, at Providence Care, we were dealing with a nurse who was suddenly not charting correctly the way they had been for so long. I knew I had a problem to fix (and not a decision to make), because they were once charting as needed. With that determined, we began by asking *what has changed?* and went to the Problem Pane to determine which of the quadrants the problem fit in. Did this nurse not know, did they not have the ability, not have the tools, or simply not care? Maybe it wasn't a matter of them not caring. Maybe a computer glitch led to the nurse's charts not being saved as they always had and they were unaware that it was happening. The latter was indeed the case. Remember that sometimes computers and technologies don't perform as needed and tools break down.

Through reasoning and deduction, your job is to correctly identify the root cause of why the problem occurred and prescribe a fitting remedy. Problem-solving can be hard, but it doesn't have to be complicated. Let this matrix be your key problem-solving asset, so you are never again left misdiagnosing problems and wondering why you can't find the answers. Everything can be solved systematically.

Consistency is key. That happens when you identify and document the habits that are working, set up the systems, follow great processes, and hire great people to run them. Given the diversity of ideas and perspectives from your team, everyone will have a slightly different system based on their title, but the key is to have one that guides! From there, all problems can become an opportunity for all involved to learn and grow from the experience.

The Key Questions

Be Smart, Be Systematic

- Know When a Problem Is Actually a Decision:
  - *When you are facing a decision, do you have a system that has worked before that you can leverage?*

    - *When you are facing a problem, how does your current process need to change?*
- Diagnose the Problem:
    - *Is what you are experiencing an exemption or the rule?*
    - *Is the problem temporary or permanent?*
    - *Is this a people problem, a product problem, or a process problem?*
- Identify the Cause and Solve the Problem:
    - *What is the root cause of the problem? How long ago did it begin? Is what you are seeing a symptom or a cause?*
    - *How can you use existing team members to facilitate problem-solving efforts?*
    - *Does the remedy to the problem coincide with your organization's core values?*

Take Action

---

1. **Perform a root cause analysis:** As we covered above, it is critical to get to the root cause to ensure your solution matches the actual problem, not just the symptoms. To reach the root of a problem—the reason it is happening—ask *why?* five times. This will help you navigate your way to the true cause.

2. **Outline your resources:** Any time you have to shape a problem-solving plan, create a table outlining the resources you need, who is going to execute accessing them, and by when. Then, match the problems to the resources. Writing out what you have at your disposal will very likely help you see that you have more available to you than you thought!

PROBLEM	CURRENT RESOURCES	BEST SUITED TO OWN IT	DEADLINE
A)	A)		
B)	B)		
C)	C)		

3. **Consider the ripple effects:** At the same time you're solving a problem, you need to be considering the side effects—the potential risks and downfalls, any change it will cause, and to whom. How will your solution affect other people or processes? What is the worst that can happen and would it be catastrophic? Does it make more sense to keep things as they are, if the treatment is deemed worse than the disease? Be sure the solution is worth it on all fronts!

When you are committed to navigating the nuances in your environment, and to moving forward with habits for success, you take the time to set up systems! Businesses and relationships are successful because they effectively solve problems and efficiently seize opportunities. This is the work you get paid for. An effective leader can fulfill both of these tasks. An exceptional leader rarely has to solve problems because they can trust in the systems and processes they have established. They can spend their time, energy, and efforts seizing the opportunities that spur growth. You can't seize new opportunities when you are constantly looking in the rear-view mirror trying to solve old problems. Without a problem-solving process in place, you will end up chasing your tail, solving the same problems over and over again.

The more problems and decisions you encounter, the more comfortable you will become navigating them. You reach a place where you see them as opportunities to grow, can embrace what is, and are able to ask effective questions to become better. Decision-making is more than a gut reaction, or a sixth sense. It's a process and sometimes an artform, and you may not have developed that skill quite yet! Be patient with yourself, it takes time. But you can be smart with every step you take. The small, unsexy, everyday decisions can add up to big success—or big failure. Follow the tactics laid out in this chapter and you can literally save yourself millions of dollars over the long term and build a culture of people who will walk through a brick wall for each other. Also, once you solve a problem, don't change what you have done just because you don't see growth immediately. Give it some time. You would never plant a crop and pull it up every two days to see if it is growing. Water it, nurture it, make sure the soil (the culture) is healthy. Even a bad plant can succeed in good soil with effective coaching, culture, and follow-through.

The first million is always the hardest.

MILESTONE 9: LEAD WITH WISDOM

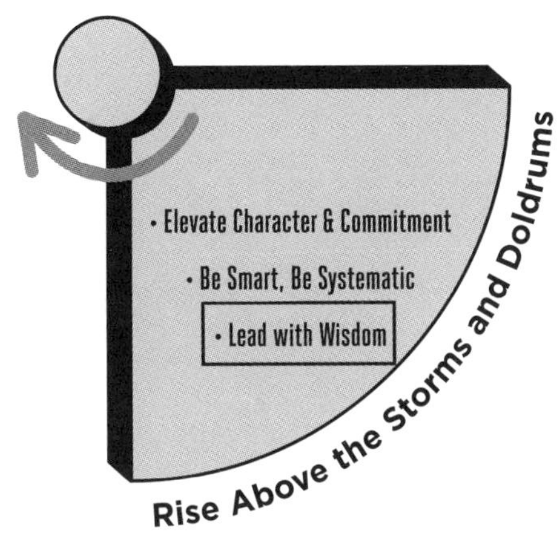

LEAD WITH WISDOM

In 1993, during my junior year of high school, my father decided to start his own business. Together, he and my mother worked six days a week toward fulfilling a vision—offering affordable housing to those who didn't have the resources to obtain a home. For my father, every day played out like Groundhog Day. He'd wake up, slam coffee down his throat, get to the office, work a ten- to twelve-hour day, and come home to plop in front of the television long enough to eat dinner, before crashing into bed. He'd wake up the next day and do it all again. It all felt depressing to me. In spite of the hours, days, weeks, and months he poured into his vision, I watched him struggle to find success. My father was relentlessly pushing ahead, yet something was missing. Everything was harder than it should be.

Often, on Saturdays and the weekdays I was off from school, I would help my father around the office. Going there together, we'd spend our thirty-minute commutes talking about the struggles he was facing. I'll never forget our conversation about millionaires and successful people. He turned to me and said, "You know, Johnnie, your first million will always be the hardest. After that they get easier." Even at seventeen, I recall thinking that what he said made sense.

In those early years, my father's goal had been to make $1,000 a day. It wasn't until five years after he started that he accomplished it, making just over $365,000 in profit that year, and giving us all something to celebrate. His conviction fascinated me, knowing he was nowhere near making $1 million yet. Why was the second million easier than the first? As I considered his words about the first million being the hardest, my mind went to the well-known saying that it takes money to make money. Having a million dollars would obviously allow for taking that money and reinvesting it in other opportunities. Then those investments would start to multiply. It was just a matter of reaching the point—that first million—for this to become a possibility. At least that was what I initially believed as a young man. Then, in the process of building Providence Care, the truth became clearer.

The reason I have come to recognize that the second, third, or even tenth million is always easier to earn than the first is not because it takes money to make money. It's also not because having a million equates to greater power or influence. The truth is that the subsequent millions become easier because you, the business owner, have changed! Things get better when you get better.

Even if making a million dollars is not your personal goal, think of your first million as being equivalent to fulfilling your first big vision. By the time you get there, your capacity and strength to hold the weight is now much stronger. When you have successfully navigated the storms and doldrums to make it to this point in your journey, you have developed your skills, became wiser, and the things that would stress you out in the beginning, barely show up on your radar. Your shoulders have grown broader and hopefully the time spent staring at the ceiling fan has decreased. Problems have grown more commonplace, and you have the systems set up to solve them, shifting your team from being reactive to proactive. What you've built starts to transform into something you don't have to be involved in as the driver leading the mission on a daily basis. Your value has increased because of the incredible value you have delivered to your team, your customers, and all of your stakeholders. You did it with clarity of what right looks like. And you were smart enough to learn from your mistakes, while building the strategic systems and processes to make everything run smoothly. That is your ninth milestone.

It does no good to have the keys but not have the wisdom to know which doors they unlock! Now, you are ready to optimize the systems that will sustain you. They will help you focus on forward progress and innovation, allowing you to capture new opportunities for scalability—so your value to the world will spread and catch fire.

You want to become more like a pair of guardrails, ensuring things remain on track from a big-picture perspective. Stepping back to act in this guiding capacity will also free you to focus more on seizing opportunities, rather than solving daily problems. My dad was unable to get to this stage with his company, but watching and learning from him allowed me to know where I didn't want to stop with Providence. True wisdom is the key to the second million and every million that follows.

What I have learned thus far about wisdom is that it has two sources: the setbacks you survive and the revelation you receive. It boils down to the difference between knowing the facts and recognizing the truths. This is the key to your sustainability. It is what will move you from simply creating or achieving an outcome to setting up the systems, process, and information sharing that give your vision and impact longevity.

Streamline Your Systems and Processes

There are likely many recurring problems within your enterprise—staffing shortages, unmotivated or distracted team members, rising prices, and product or service quality that does not meet expectations. These may even be something you and your team dismiss as normal. However, just because something is common doesn't make it normal! Cancer is common, but not normal. Don't accept what is common. The truth is that most problems are recurring, so what you need are *recurring systems* to identify the habits that work, document them, and create a culture that will follow them! You need to build a problem-mitigation process. Leaders with great wisdom understand that without this, you will always be at the mercy of your problems, instead of the problems being at the mercy of your solutions.

Early on, I believed that when I hired great people, gave them the resources and direction they needed, and got out of their way, we would all thrive. This thinking was flawed, because I left out one critical piece: the processes. Don't make the mistake that cost me millions! It's true that hiring great people is critical, as we have already covered. And you need to give them the resources and direction to thrive—and even step out of their way to allow them to do so. But between your people and the desired results there needs to be *clear processes.* Let your people run the processes and let your processes run the enterprise. That way, when good people leave you, you'll still have the processes and protection manuals to run the business in their absence. This is how you scale your vision. This is wisdom.

You will not be able to innovate or grow if you are constantly solving problems the wrong way, stuck in the weeds, or fighting just to get back to zero. Processes—how you effectively execute and manage your systems—are the key to freeing you up. They will allow you to seize opportunities and expand your vision. One of the most effective ways to do this is to create operations manuals that highlight the delegation, processes, standards, and templates that help keep everyone singing from the same page. Categorize and simplify everything you do. Break your problems and decisions down to their simplest form and bring them into focus, so they can be easily and consistently solved. Here is how the process of streamlining your systems should play out:

1. **Define the need:** Is what you are facing a problem or an opportunity? What are you trying to accomplish? Name the problem or opportunity and its corresponding outcome. This *[position, etc.]* is successful when *[____________]* is achieved at *[insert date]*? Clarity will give you power. To identify how to make your systems more efficient and effective, reverse-engineer the question *how can you help your clients or customers have a better day?* This includes templates for running meetings or making follow-up calls.

2. **Change the way you define roles:** Instead of simply being a job description, every role needs to include the outcomes accomplished when success is realized. Create job descriptions with specific outcomes that are identified with daily, weekly, monthly, quarterly, biannual, and annual results. You are paying for outcomes, not attempts! In plain, straightforward language, list what you want the outcomes of every team member and team to be. What does right look like? For example, "If this committee were completely successful, we would have accomplished *[____________]*." The next question will then become: *What will it take to achieve these outcomes?*
3. **Create a protection or operations manual**, and update it annually: Take note of your best employees—those who have gotten the closest to their desired outcomes. What do they do on a consistent basis? What does right look like for them? What are their outcomes? Document their functions and touch points—when they do their tasks and how long it takes. Break them down into daily, weekly, bi-weekly, monthly, and annual duties. Include templates, checklists, and other tools, such as an appendix of how to run your meetings. Describe how to execute every technical aspect of every job. Until you have created the manual for a position, don't hire to fill it! This is your blueprint for remaining aligned with what right looks like long-term.

4. **Make your team a resource:** While you can be the ultimate designer of manuals, let your team be an untapped reservoir of input and new operational ideas on which you can capitalize. The further you are up the leadership chain, the less you see the cause and effect, because you are not working on front lines. Once your manual is established, let your team do the heavy lifting! Even when your manual isn't perfect and requires evolution over time, the presence of such a system is going to get you closer to the desired outcome and support the sustainability and scalability of your vision.
5. **Create and regularly access an operations calendar:** At the back of your operations manual, detail a twelve-month calendar of the processes and systems that work—what needs to be done, when, and why. This should be married with any strategic plan and budget for that role or department for every year. The calendar needs to contain the key touch points and timelines for completing duties. Print off a calendar for every department, every quarter. At your annual general meeting, have your department heads review the manual and update what needs to be changed due to changes in your environment. Have division leaders responsible for the outcomes and dissemination of their strategic plans, to ensure that all departments are synchronized.

6. **Track progress through scorecards:** Twice a month, your team members and their division leaders should come together to review and reflect how they are doing in relation to their strategic calendar. This can be achieved by grading themselves on templated scorecards that highlight the specific goals detailed in the outcomes for their role. This system can be as simple as using stoplight colors: when you are red, you are at a full stop; when you are yellow, things are slowing down; when you are green, things are moving forward in alignment with outcomes. Meet with your top-line people on a weekly basis to talk about where they are with their scorecards. Compiling data is critical. Make sure everyone on your team knows how to interpret it and what to do with it. It's easy to beat the data to death and make it say what you want, but that won't do you any good if you intend to keep growing! Proper interpretation is critical.
7. **Always manage according to the manual:** When you are holding meetings, there should never be a performance-related conversation without referencing your operations manual! Have it become everyone's touch point. Hardwire your touchpoints and the recurring processes needed to create a high-quality, predictable experience for your team and customers.

When you are serious about what you are doing, you take the time to set up systems! When you are wise, you simplify, streamline, and make everything more efficient. Efficiency happens internally, effectiveness happens externally—in the marketplace. Leaders and directors focus on effectiveness; front-line workers focus on efficiency by looking closely at the components and simplifying them.

When it comes to shaping your processes, your whole leadership team needs to be on the same page; every team member needs to be on board. It may seem harder to focus on simplifying your systems in the short term, but doing so will always be beneficial in the long term. Working hard does not have to be complicated. When you are truly committed to navigating the nuances in your environment and to forging habits and rituals for success, then you will do this work. Without this crucial step in wisdom, you will always be the bottleneck, constantly having to manage, adjust, or reinvent yourself.

Don't Sit Down

Think of your progress like climbing a ladder. As you have risen, rung by rung, things likely have felt unstable at times. It might be daunting to look down and see how far you could fall, or look up and see how much climbing remains. Then, as your vision is being fulfilled, you encounter something new. Standing on the highest rung, there is nowhere to rest. Despite having the people and processes in place that allow you to sit down, you can't! You may feel the need to take a breath, but you can't take long, because sustained growth and success must remain the focus.

The journey is far from over; you have a team and customers depending on you! At this point, you likely find yourself in what I like to call the *yes now but not yet* phase. This means you have arrived at a certain point or milestone on your journey, but you have not yet reached your ultimate destination. You may be having a better day than yesterday, but there is still much room to grow. Leadership will always be a battle of focus between the here-and-now and the not-quite-yet! It's in this dance that true leaders are made. Now that you have problem-solving processes in place, you want to be focused on doing what will sustain you for the long term, even with your decisions in the moment. This means you never stop learning, gaining insight, and innovating—putting your wisdom into action.

Business has two potential directions: expansion or contraction. If you rest to the point of stopping, you are inevitably going to contract. You are only ever as successful as your last best customer experience, so you must continue to evolve. The question you ask yourself now needs to be *is this all there is?* After each problem you conquer, you can't just go back to where you were prior to facing it; you need to use the setback as an opportunity to stretch beyond! The goal must always be to become stronger, seeing that every problem you faced has granted you the opportunity for perspective. Knowing that perspective is the beginning of wisdom. In order to not sit still, you must ask the questions that challenge the status quo:

- *How can your vision grow to become more impactful than yesterday?*
- *How do you serve more people?*
- *What season is your industry in and where will it be in the next three years? What are the regulatory and law challenges that may or may not come?*

- *What is one step you can take today to get ahead of the curve* (assuming you have identified the curve)?

Bring the following questions to your team and investigate your current offer together:

- *Are you still at the cutting edge of what is happening in your industry?*
- *What would the outcome be if you had to achieve the same level of production or service in half the time? What would change? What would not?*
- *What questions should you be asking that you don't know to ask? What is your blind spot?*
- *If you didn't exist tomorrow, would your customers care?* (This one kept me up at night.)

Sometimes the biggest hurt a team or enterprise can suffer is success, because it removes the hunger. Having a healthy level of paranoia can push you to not sit down. When Providence Care was making tens of millions a year and serving thousands of patients, I would always manage as if we were broke. Doing so kept us pushing toward growth. Success can breed complacency and laziness. You can't afford to become apathetic (nor can your brand), because you will fall behind and be overtaken by your competition and what you built won't be sustained. If you think of achieving your goal as a garden, you are likely enjoying the fruits of your labor at this point, but as we discussed, seasons change. So do the conditions in which you must continue to tend your garden. Weeds always grow, and competition is always at the perimeter trying to steal and eat your crops.

At this point, just as it was when you began, vision is about looking beyond where the eyes can see—over the horizon and to the unsuspecting spaces in between. Ask bigger questions and you'll get bigger answers. At Providence Care, my questions changed from, "How can I get a patient," to "How can I touch and serve every single South Carolinian who has a two-year or less life expectancy?" When your questions change, your strategy changes as well. Successful leaders have the ability to do all this, knowing there is nothing safe about remaining static, and that every problem and experience produces wisdom, when you're willing to look at it in its totality. It's your job to see the 30,000-foot view and bring that back to your team.

Open More Doors to the House of *Yes*

What is the one word you want to hear from your potential customer after making an offer? The word is *Yes*! Yes to doing business with you. And what is one common aspect the best brands have? They all have more than one product or service to sell. They all have more than one door to enter the house of *yes*. So should you! When you think about adding more services or products, you don't begin by asking *does this make us money?* But rather by making your first question *does this create massive value?* If the answer is *yes,* then ask how you can you monetize it to make it a sustainable offer.

As Providence Care found itself having to meet ever-changing Medicare regulations, a large segment of our market was being left without coverage. Rules stipulated that patients couldn't undergo both chemotherapy and hospice care simultaneously, leaving us seemingly unable to help those who chose to undergo intensive treatments and therapies. We had to figure out how to sustain our vision to serve the underserved. The idea of leaving these people behind did not sit well with our team, so we started a non-hospice pain and symptom control division. We innovated at the bedside, not in the boardroom, by taking care of what the patients said they wanted and desperately needed. We started Providence House Calls to provide at-home care. We hired physicians and nurse practitioners, training them to become experts in pain and symptom management. We visited patients who weren't willing to give up their therapies or treatments and remained in need of pain and symptom relief. We would help them reconcile their medications and make sure their pain and symptoms were under control, so they'd be better able to tolerate their treatments. While we received insufficient Medicare reimbursement for these services, they quickly led to a newfound reputation of being the healthcare company that would not say *no*. In an industry known for telling patients *sorry, there is nothing else we can do*, we were the ones saying *yes, we can help*.

Hospital at Home was another entry point to our house of *yes*! But it was up to us to figure out how to sustain it. As a rebirth of our agency was taking hold, everything had to come back to our mission and vision. The vision remained the same but greater. If we were in the business of changing lives, then the decision to pursue both home-based palliative and chronic care management made sense.

We grew a program that allowed us to rebrand our entire company to what would become known as our region's only Hospital at Home service provider. It included physician house calls, home health, non-hospice palliative medicine, and end-of-life hospice care, all under one roof. It became a one-stop shop for ambulatory care for patients sick enough to be hospitalized yet stable enough for in-home care. We were achieving greater outcomes with less money and reinventing ourselves in an industry that was past due for disruption. We didn't shift the direction or destination; we just broadened our scope.

For the first three to four years, our expanded ventures weren't financially sustainable. In order to make it stand the test of time, we started a nonprofit to help maintain it; any loss was offset by profits made in our other lines of service. Within three years of executing great management, logistics, and processes, we made our new offer profitable. In time, we even achieved over half a million a year in profit with something that initially seemed unprofitable. Even if it didn't make us a lot of money, there was no denying that it created a lot of value for our patients. It also granted us the opportunity to touch more people and change even more lives—which was always the foremost goal. We weren't in the hospice business any longer; we were in the changing lives business and our business exploded because of it.

There are only two real choices at this point in your journey: disrupt or die. It's as simple as that. Innovation boils down to expanding your identity—redefining and expanding the business you are really in versus the one you thought you were in. While continuing to solve today's problems, with your streamlined processes and your team carrying the weight, aim to be at the forefront of your industry. This happens not by changing what you do, but becoming better at it and offering it in a new way.

There are two types of innovation: internal (the efficiency of your systems and processes, which we covered earlier) and external, which encompasses the questions:

- *What business are you in?*
- *What business are you really in? (The core business?)*
- *What businesses should you be in?*

Here is a secret for you: If you are in the business of truly serving others' interests instead of your own, you will be profoundly successful due to the lack of competition. With this in mind, what can your vision now become?

When you look back at how long it took you and your enterprise to reach this point, it should be clear how much your industry and environment have changed. As people's wants, needs, and desires evolve, you need to ask if you are still meeting them. When you are not, the way out is to continue to innovate. Whether through internal processes and external products or services, it is critical to have multiple doors to your house of *yes*. This means when people say no to joining in your vision with your front door offer, offer them the back entrance or even a window! Give prospective customers multiple ways to become involved in your vision. This means starting with the question of how you create more value, followed by how you can monetize it—in that order:

- *Who is adding more value than you in your industry? How are they doing it? Why are they doing it?* Define their attributes and then apply them to yourself and your enterprise internally. Once you hit those attributes, expand upon them.

- *Are your current systems allowing you to solve problems effectively? If not, how can you simplify even further?*
- *What could be added to your systems and processes? Is there a missing link that could catapult your enterprise to the next level and increase your levels of service?*
- *What can you do to create an ecosystem that will sustain itself?* (Like Providence Care's nonprofit to sustain the palliative care division.)

Look back at what you did to get where you are, identify the success points, and then apply them to your new doors to the house of *yes*. New voices, new people, and new questions can all feed into your innovation efforts. Engage in expansive conversations and allow new voices to enter the room. Evoke new thought on what you can be doing, and develop more of that salt-and-pepper passion we talked about when bringing on new team members. If you keep going to the same people, you are going to continue to get the same ideas.

Expand your point of view, and be sure to continuously stretch your own mind—ask who you have to become to make your enterprise more sustainable. Do the inside work that attracts what you want externally. This is a tale of continuous innovation, not something you do as a novelty. Aim to create added value and be the first. Be the one everyone else is looking at! As an added bonus, when you're the one making changes in your environment, you won't have to worry about changes in your industry shaping you. Initiate the shift to open a new door and you'll quickly see how all previous truths and rules change and everyone in the implementation process starts back at ground zero. This will bring with it new thought and fresh ways of viewing a particular problem or situation.

The Key Questions

Lead with Wisdom

- Streamline Your Systems and Processes:
  - *What are your key recurring problems?*
  - *How can you streamline and communicate processes to address them?*
- Don't Sit Down:
  - *Are you solving yesterday's problems or tomorrow's?*
  - *Are you capitalizing on yesterday's opportunities or tomorrow's?*
- Open More Doors to the House of *Yes*:
  - *How does your team perceive you as it relates to your acceptance of new ideas? Do you embrace innovation or do you have your mind already made up for what works and what doesn't?*
  - *Are there other services or products that complement your offerings? How could you integrate them into your organization?*

Take Action

1. **Sound like a broken record:** Sometimes I am asked "How many times do I have to tell them?" My answer is the same every time: repeat your processes and outcomes over and over! When you feel sick of saying it, and are ready to bang your head against the wall, congratulations, that's likely the first time some of your team have truly heard it.
2. **Duplicate the best:** Volunteer outside of your industry, start reading publications from other fields. Listen to well-regarded podcasts. Then ask yourself how you can relate what you learn to what you are doing in *your* industry. Find three industries outside of yours and identify the key attribute leading companies have that enable them to rise above their competitors. Customize and implement those attributes within your team.
3. **Surpass the success of others as you differentiate:** Attend national industry conferences and track the curve of business—with insight to be able to see what's coming around the corner. Follow the success that others have made. Once you arrive at the same place as they have, chart your own success by customizing your internal processes and capturing the opportunities that are unique to your industry and outside the norm. Pass those processes along to your team to help fuel a culture of expansion.

It's worth repeating that success should never be a surprise, nor should failure. Every enterprise is perfectly designed and managed for the results they are getting. If you are getting great results, congratulations and keep going. If not, it's time to get wise and reassess. Success will always be a lagging indicator—a byproduct of what you have done six to twelve months ago. The same is true of failure—the result of what you *didn't* do. The more you experience with eyes wide open, the wiser you will continue to become.

For those who like formulas here is one: the longer you persevere, the greater your character becomes. The greater your character, the greater your wisdom. With wisdom, comes perspective; and with a wise perspective, you increase your likelihood of finding joy and fulfillment—the ultimate point where you want your journey to land. Gaining wisdom is not about knowing everything and always making the correct decisions. It's about being able to ask deeper questions and gain foresight. Like the success you seek, wisdom is a process, never a destination. Life is constantly happening for you, so long as you see it that way. Simplify your systems and processes, never sit down, and constantly innovate. Be a resource for continued growth.

MAKE IT SUSTAINABLE

What you are given and who you become is for you, but it's not really for you!

MILESTONE 10: TRANSFORM SUCCESS INTO SIGNIFICANCE

TRANSFORM SUCCESS INTO SIGNIFICANCE

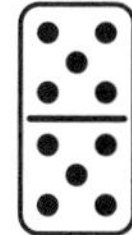

At the completion of our regular monthly orientations with the new members of the Providence Care team, the last part of my slide deck had three pictures of bodies of water in Israel. The first was the sixty-four-square-mile Sea of Galilee. It is a magical, biblically associated freshwater lake over 680 feet below sea level in the great depression of the Jordan River Valley. It is home to majestic birds, fertile soil, fish, and lush greenery growing nearby. Thanks to its sheltered location, low elevation, and the influence of the lake itself, mild winters promote the cultivation of bananas, dates, citrus fruit, and other vegetables. It is everything and more that you would expect from a beautiful body of water that thrives with life.

The second image was that of the Dead Sea, a well-known salt lake in the desert between Israel and Jordan, seated between the hills of Judaea to the west and the Transjordanian plateaus to the east. With a surface elevation of 1,410 feet below sea level, it is the lowest body of water on the planet. The lake is an abundant source of salt, with most of its southern basin subdivided into dozens of large evaporation pools. It all began when heavy water flowed into the lake, depositing thick sediments of shale, clay, sandstone, rock salt and gypsum. The dramatic reduction of the inflow of water beginning in the 1960s only gradually increased the salinity of the upper-layer waters, amplifying this effect. To this day, as most of us know, the waters of the Dead Sea remain extremely saline, drawing crowds of bathers who bask in their ability to stay afloat without moving. However, any excitement tied to the lake's surroundings is a stark contrast to the Sea of Galilee.

To cap it off, I would share a final picture of the 233-mile-long Jordan River. Sitting in a structural depression, the river rises on the slopes of Mount Hermon, on the border between Syria and Lebanon, flowing south through northern Israel, where it finds the Sea of Galilee. Passing through that body of water, it then continues southward, eventually emptying into the Dead Sea. What is most interesting is that the Jordan River is the source of water for both the Sea of Galilee and the Dead Sea—two vastly different bodies! My question for new team members is always: *If both lakes share the same source of water, why is one dead and the other alive?*

The answer is that the Sea of Galilee gives away all that it receives, and the Dead Sea keeps everything for itself! When the Jordan River passes through the Sea of Galilee, it allows life to come in and flow out of it. The Dead Sea, on the other hand, is an endpoint, holding on to everything the Jordan River has brought it. The lesson of this illustration is that in order to flourish and to continue to receive, like the Sea of Galilee, *you must give it away*!

This is what is meant by what you are given and who you become is *for you*, but also *not really for you*!

You cannot pour into a full cup. When you hold on to everything yourself, you won't be able to take on anything else and you will stagnate. There will be no room for growth. Giving it away has to do with emptying yourself by allowing what you have received—money, wisdom, knowledge, and being present as a leader—to flow *through* you and not just *to* you. It is much like the saying *die empty.* Leaders should lead empty, pouring out everything you have to others. When you learn something, give it to someone else. It was for you, but also not for you. It is for everyone who has built the enterprise alongside you and for those whose lives you continue to work to make better through your work.

As a leader or founder, you can have it all without holding on to it all. When you release what you no longer need to hold on to and empower your team to take things from here, you are making room for new opportunities, for personal growth, and to focus on making those around you even better leaders. The only path to receiving more is by continuously creating room, while remaining open to growth—even when you think you have already learned and shared it all! You are planting healthy seeds and disrupting failure in a way like never before. By this point in your journey, not only has your environment changed; you have as well. It is time to step into your next level and rise from mere success to significance and impact—the definition of true success. This is your tenth milestone.

Serve Outside Your Lines

When you seek to create value for others first, the growth will always come back to you in ways you will never plan for or expect.

At a time when Providence Care's growth had allowed for the agency to give back to the community in new and bigger ways, I read about an opportunity gap with minority nurses in the state of South Carolina. It was clear what Providence Care needed to do. Quickly, our leadership team came together and dedicated scholarship awards for qualified minorities who wanted to pursue degrees to become registered nurses. The grant would cover a percentage of their tuition. We did this because we wanted to contribute outside of our lines and into the larger community.

Upon graduation, some of these nurses went on to work in geriatric or acute care settings. What we never expected was that when it came time for their patients to need end-of-life care, guess what company's name would come up as who they would want to call? Providence Care. Why? Because this was an echo of our impact on others. This is the *give it away* principle in action.

Being able to serve more patients was an unintentional result of offering the scholarships (nor could we have predicted it). It would never have happened if we hadn't made the choice to give things away in the name of expanding our impact. The needs of thousands of our patients and of our team were always prioritized on a daily basis. That never stopped. And yet, when I look back at the most memorable moments, amid countless touching encounters with our patients and their families, what stood out was the children in need whom we sponsored, the food drives and winter coat collections we participated in, or the meals our team cooked for patients.

Fulfillment and significance lie in the seas of contribution and growth. Self-actualization and becoming the best version of yourself stem from giving back and having realized success for yourself and your team. When you have seen success, it is not time to sit back and enjoy your pie; you are here to help a larger market bake more pies! You are needed to become a catalyst for disrupting failure on a larger scale. Instead of simply sharing a slice of your pie, you must at times be willing to give away the entire recipe to whomever needs it. This step is about helping the next person have things a little bit easier than you.

Serving outside your lines means ensuring that you look for more ways to touch lives, internally and externally. Become a force for good in the community in a way that amplifies and extends the boundaries of the culture you created, making your enterprise a place where people want to become involved in your vision. This is about fueling a situation of *yes and*, not *either or.* Ask yourself such questions as:

- *Who else can benefit from the impact you create?*
- *What do you need to keep doing or to expand upon it?*
- *How can you further contribute to the growth and joy of your team members? What does that involve?*

You started with a vision for yourself and brought in others who believed in it. You invested in others with knowledge, skill and relationships. But now you have reached the point where it is clear that *it was for you, but not really for you.* Real personal growth happens when you stop and think about the echo of your impact. Your outcome as a leader should always be your impact in changing the lives of other human beings and helping to shape a team who can lead themselves. Your job is to be a mirror that reflects the potential of others, while teaching them to ask the questions that will help them grow. As you help, their ideas and passions become fused with your own, making the vision for what you are creating become bigger than before. It also becomes bigger than you! Consider the similarity to a new, devoted marriage where each spouse has a vision for what the marriage could ultimately become. However, neither of their visions are complete until they have been shared with someone—a partner. The most successful of these partnerships are those where there is a literal marriage of shared visions and shared ideas, where the original visions became greater than any one person could have created on their own.

Become the Least Important Person in the Room

Ten years into building Providence Care, we found ourselves in our prime, enjoying our best year to date. We had accomplished and overcome so much, grown to more than two hundred employees and three offices, were serving thousands of patients every day, and were touching many thousands more families. Our focus was on the quality of care and ensuring we always met regulations—after surmounting that $1.8 million learning curve with Medicare. We weren't the biggest agency, nor were we aiming to be. We simply continued to aim to be the best at what we did: overserving the underserved.

Just as we felt as though we had found our groove and things were buzzing along, the COVID-19 pandemic hit, bringing with it an influx of new regulations. People who chose not to be vaccinated could cost us two percent of our Medicare coverage. Doctor's offices stopped seeing patients. Long-term care facilities went into lockdown, and mask mandates swept over the entire industry. Even with all of this fear and trepidation, it was incredible to watch our team dive in, adjusting to the new dynamics, all while always holding true to our values. People from different backgrounds, viewpoints, faiths, and all religions were intentional on turning *to each other* while it seemed the world was turning *on* each other. No one was criticized for choosing to wear or not wear a mask. What was going on in the bigger picture of society seemed to come to an abrupt halt at the doors of Providence Care. At a time when there was a great influx of policy changes, we found ourselves coming together and returning to our values, and the focus remained on our patients and supporting each other even through our differences and fears.

Sharing what you have gained requires humility and trust in your team, culture, and systems. When I would show up to meetings, I would ask the team what we needed to do based on the latest mandates or the most recent environmental changes. I knew my team was now in charge, and I had confidence that everyone involved had our patients' best interests at heart. At times, I would walk in and almost feel as though I was holding the team back, as if I had become a bottleneck that they continuously had to get up to date. Although I retained authority, I was no longer in direct control, which led to more personal freedom for me.

It was clear that I had achieved what I had set out to do: I had finally become the least important person in the room. It was a realization that led to mixed feelings dancing inside of me. I was thankful, relieved, and proud that our matured team was able to come together and find a way through tumultuous times. I was humbled and grateful for everything they had co-labored to create. But it wasn't easy to feel as though I was no longer needed. I had worked myself out of a job, which was clearly evident when I would show up to the office in a t-shirt and a ball cap without question from anyone around me. That year, I had never worked in the business so little. My time had been spent working on PR opportunities—the shaking people's hands and kissing babies part. I was focused on seizing opportunities by opening more doors to the house of *yes*.

You must realize that at this stage, if the business is still dependent on you, you have created a job for yourself, not a sustainable team or enterprise. You need to have given your team the tools and wisdom to execute the vision you built, opening up the space for you to move from working *in* the business to focusing *on* the business. It's time to step away from solving recurring problems and focus on the next opportunity to seize, while still showing up at company functions in a "shaking hands and kissing babies" capacity. This is your return to the people part of the business.

In the previous chapter, I spoke about setting up the systems, processes, and knowledge-sharing that allow your team to run the show while you move to acting like the guardrails—sitting back, observing, and guiding the bigger picture. When you first launched your vision, you had to show up in a big way to keep everything moving forward. Now, the tables have turned and you want to be able to not show up, while also having confidence that things will continue to progress without you.

A team or enterprise is never intended to be led from the top down. You built your vision from the bottom up and now that foundation has grown strong enough to sustain the operation without you. Becoming the least important person in the room means you are stepping deeper into a new evolution of your leadership and realizing the next level of contribution within your enterprise.

As you have expanded a shared vision and weathered storms together, your team members have all been on their own individual journeys. They have grown their character and commitment just as you have. Now, you must make the decision whether to hold them back, by continuing to manage everything, or release them and let them grow. As the tide of the next phase of your journey washes in, all boats should rise. Everyone is dealing with their own significance. You want to empower them to rise to the occasion by giving them the tools they need and by stepping back to allow them to execute—and trusting that they can do so. This is the watershed effect leadership can have on others.

When you have followed the principles of this book, you likely:

- Have built a leadership team that reflects your values and collectively makes better decisions than you alone ever could.
- Have shaped a team that is dedicated to following the processes and protection manual, updating them on an annual basis.
- Are helping more and more people and changed countless lives.
- Are as profitable as ever.
- Have created an environment of shared ownership throughout the enterprise for both success and failures.
- Have become a learning organization, where everyone has the right to teach and share their experiences and opinions for the betterment of the whole. Everyone is showing up authentically and is fully aligned with the greater vision.

Now here's the catch: becoming the least important person in the room is a lagging indicator of countless efforts, not a result of doing something in the moment or a decision you instantaneously make. It's like going to the gym regularly and seeing greater strength and muscles develop gradually. Like many of us, your vision and confidence may have built over time, through daily actions over the course of many years. And then all at once, you're walking into a meeting one day, wearing a t-shirt and ball cap. You're feeling like you need to be caught up to speed by your team on the fantastic progress they've been making. You suddenly realize that it's time to step back and assess:

- *Have you become the bottleneck?*
- *Is your season as a leader in your current role changing?*
- *Have you arrived at this point feeling like a greater version of yourself? Does that translate into you being ready to step into the next phase of you growing your vision or giving it away?*

I have heard countless patients at the end of their lives talk about the good stuff: service, relationships, and contribution. It's the same at this level of your leadership development. When what you have built is all about you, you haven't created a successful, sustainable team. If you have answered *yes* to the above questions, congratulations, you have reached the next fork in the road. You are ready to reassess what's most important for you and your leadership.

If you haven't answered *yes*, it's important to ensure you haven't become the least important person in the room to the detriment of the team! What I mean is, don't create senseless pursuits that keep you busy, yet deter your team members from doing their job. And don't keep changing the focus by introducing the next new or special project of the week—created to help break your boredom while searching for something to make you feel as important as you did during the days when you made all the decisions. Innovation is great, but never at the detriment of your team. You're beyond that now. It's okay that you are no longer the stained-glass window with the sun casting magically through it that receives all the attention, because now you are the cornerstone.

Reassess What's Important

Kelley and I love to frequent Steak 48 in Charlotte. She gets the steak and I get the lobster, along with all of the fixings—bruschetta, wine, dessert. Every time we eat there, I leave feeling full and satisfied. The best part of a great dining experience (and what makes it great) is knowing when to stop. You can love on cookies all day long, but you will quickly reach a point of diminishing returns. The second cookie might not quite taste as good as the first, and the third, fourth, or fifth will surely begin to lose their allure. Keep going beyond the point of enjoyment and you'll have turned a great meal or favorite treat into something that is no longer enjoyable. Wisdom is knowing that one is good, but two doesn't always equal twice as good.

With the vantage point of success behind you, you get to ask the necessary questions to determine if you are ready to recommit to the degree needed to take your enterprise to the next level. Do you eat the next cookie or order the extra side to your steak or lobster dinner, or is it time to find a new favorite indulgence? Reassessing what's important is an essential piece in the fulfillment/significance equation. It is also critical to realizing the full potential of your vision. Doing so should run in parallel to giving back outside your lines and becoming the least important person in the room.

In order to continue with your current vision, you need to double down and give what you gave before all over again. Are you ready for that? You may feel ready to commit to a new, next-level vision for your enterprise, or perhaps you are ready to give everything away by moving into a new role. Now is the time to decide if you want to continue or if you are ready to take the off-ramp. You have arrived at the point of being all you could be and doing all you could do. Are you satiated or is there still more hunger to satisfy? Only you know what you feel. Notice I said feel, because you can justify anything *with your head*, but you need to make sure your *heart* continues to follow. To grant yourself the required space to reassess, get quiet and get with your family and friends. Ask yourself the following:

- *Have you accomplished your greatest idea or beyond?*
- *Did you live up to the potential of the vision you had?*
- *Are you still excited about it all?*
- *Are you willing to walk through another day with that same or an expanded vision?*
- *Is there a different set of problems you want to solve?*
- *Are you still in season as the leader of your enterprise? Or are you prepared for a new season in your leadership journey?*

Everything comes back to your vision, how well you have fulfilled it, what you need to do to continue, and how you feel about it all! While these questions may initially feel connected to your current enterprise, the truth is that you are really addressing what is evolving in your personal world, beyond the enterprise. That's the difference between success and significance. The process of doing the work to check in with what you want will inevitably lead you to fall into one of two places:

1. **You remain hungry:** You still have that burning desire within you to create a better tomorrow for those you serve. Throw in an extra side along with your regular lobster dinner, because you still have room and remain motivated by what you are doing! Having made it this far, you still feel excited about entering your next level. Things have only just gotten started, because you know your *why* remains much bigger than any challenges you will face in making the next level a reality for your enterprise.
2. **You are fulfilled:** Your emotional cup is full in all of the best ways and it may be time to exit and literally give it all away—your title, your focus, your contributions to date. This is the case when you feel you are moving into a new season. Whether or not you have attained fulfillment of your entire vision, you get to determine how much further you want to continue walking down this same path.

These two sentiments will then lead you to two options:

1. **Grow:** You may have built a spaceship to get you to the moon, but now you have to be able to go to Mars, and you need a better ship and more supplies. Growth at this phase means questioning if you want to expand in your current lane or go somewhere else. If you remain hungry, you are ready to become the next highest version of yourself in the environment that you have created. Everything must begin with vision, even now. What will be your newly expanded destination, and what will you need to get there? Maybe you will expand to open new locations, serve new customers, or lead more people. Look at what your industry is demanding that it didn't a few years ago; ask yourself what you need to do to adapt. These inquiries will reveal what needs to be added to your enterprise in order to grow.
2. **Give it away:** Fulfillment is found in giving to other people. It is about having impact on a greater level than what you get paid to do. If you are full, you are willing to leave behind the best of yourself, so that others can grow into and give the best of themselves. As Providence Care expanded from serving hundreds of patients to caring for thousands, our bottom line exceeded the healthiest in the industry, and our competition had begun mimicking our programs and modeling our processes. The industry at large was also shifting. With post-COVID fallout, an aging population, and consolidation within the greater

healthcare industry, it felt like new doors of opportunity had begun to close.

At a time when it could have felt like things were contracting, I found my greatest fulfillment in sponsoring local youth baseball teams, the Christmas Wish fundraiser, and cooking meals for our patients. Was I still excited about our vision? Honestly, not as much, given the new need to grow bigger or go home. There was no drive to become national or the biggest; it had just always been about being the most disruptive, innovative, and impactful. The industry adjusted to our new paradigm of providing care for everyone who needed it. We were able to touch patients we had never met, due to the increased care they were receiving from our competitors—those who had to innovate to keep up with us. It felt like a vision fulfilled and a mission accomplished. In parallel, my appetite was changing and I had begun wanting something different, something new. Giving it all away may mean handing over your role to someone else or selling your enterprise. Doing so may be necessary in order to allow for room in your cup. In my case, I chose to sell and exit the adventure. The more important question is: *what will your decision be?*

The best thing you can do to determine whether you are hungry or fulfilled is to revisit the questions you asked yourself when you first began to shape your vision into a reality and make the unseen seen:

- *Does what you envision reverberate when you feel it in your soul? Does the destination feel worth the pursuit?*
- *Is this undeniably your passion?*
- *Is this the role you would wake up every day and do for free?*
- *Is this who you see yourself being?*

When you can no longer answer these questions with the same affirmative energy you did when you started, then it is time to begin asking yourself new questions or thinking of the original questions in a different capacity:

- *What is your new vision? Where is it you want to go?*
- *Who could you become in the process of pursuing this vision?*
- *What would happen if you did nothing?*
- *How do you need to show up (who do you need to be, and in what role) in order to make this a reality?*

Allow yourself the time to reassess, but never stop. You need to keep things going, whether that means you bringing in new ideas and fueling growth, or handing them off to a new leader. The first rule of success is to not go backwards. You don't want to lose what you've already gained. At this point, in order to achieve true fulfillment and significance, reassessing where you are, where your team or enterprise is, and what you want is critical.

Going forward, question if you are prepared for what is needed from you. The enterprise will progress with or without you, thanks to the vision, culture, and systems you have established. Now it's about what you are being truly called to do.

The Key Questions

Transform Success into Significance

- Serve Outside Your Lines:
  - *What have you come to value most for yourself and for your enterprise? How can you expand on that?*
  - *What is the potential you see in your team members? How can you help harness that? What are their weaknesses and how can you help your team overcome them?*
- Become the Least Important Person in the Room:
  - *What is your true value to your team? Are you a resource only being pulled in for the exceptions—when everything else is running smoothly by the rules and systems you have established?*
  - *Where are your team's chokeholds? What is holding you back? If nothing, can you get out of the way?*
- Reassess What's Important:
  - *Where is your passion and heart now versus where it was when you started?*
  - *Are you personally fulfilled to the point where you are willing to shift to a new direction?*

Take Action

1. **Be decisive with saying *yes*:** At this point, you will likely have visibility in your community. There may be charities and other organizations calling upon you for support. Saying *yes* to everyone can detract from your vision; there is power in being decisive about sponsorships and contributions. Make sure each opportunity speaks to the vision of the team you created.
2. **Hire to replace yourself:** Your number one job is to now have created something that can run without you, making your job irrelevant. You've been building toward this all along; now you get to assess how well you have done. Have you hired in a way where your people are fully running your systems, processes, and procedures? If not, what can you do to make this the case?
3. **Do a hunger check:** Do you remain hungry or are you feeling fulfilled and potentially ready for new opportunities? Check your gut. Then, after checking in with yourself, ask the people who are significant to you (family and friends) if they remain hungry with you! You will need your cheerleaders alongside you on the next path you choose.

Giving away is different than sharing. When you give something away, you have released it with trust for others to carry it on.

When you share, you retain it while also imparting it to others. Sharing what you know multiplies the impact of the knowledge, process, or wisdom that has brought you to the point of success; others now have it to use and build upon. It is not a zero-sum game. When you contribute the capacity success has granted you to your team and to larger community, your impact multiplies. You will reach more people. Giving and sharing do not diminish you in any way. They allow those around you to have more, as you become a catalyst for growth in a new way. Having built your vision into a team, shaped your culture, established systems, sold, streamlined your processes, and opened more doors to the house of *yes*, this is your next step.

Everything you have built and experienced has come *through you*, not from you. That's why giving it away or sharing it should not be seen as an impossible feat. It was never yours to begin with. As I would always tell my team, *it is for you, but it's not for you*! There is joy in giving. You have reached the point where you can become the Sea of Galilee—a clean vessel that allows things to come through you, knowing they are not for you. Live off the overflow. Bask in your taking the step from having created success to shaping an imprint of significance. Don't leave your vision simply because you are tired; move on only when you are fulfilled.

Change happens instantly. The commitment to change can take a lifetime.

MILESTONE 11:
IT MATTERS HOW YOU GET THERE

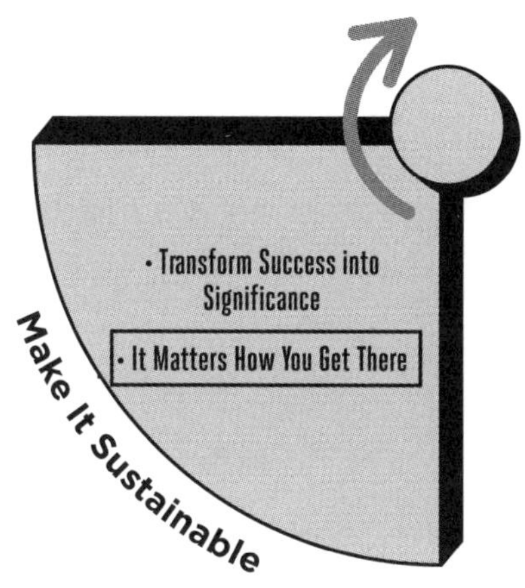

IT MATTERS HOW YOU GET THERE

What do people say about you behind your back after you leave the room? That is your legacy. You may have opted to read this book in its entirety before launching your vision. You may also be reading it in the thick of things, on day two or year twenty, in the midst of choosing to pass on the reins for your role or expand upon your initial vision. Wherever you find yourself in the journey from vision to fulfilling your destination, *it matters how you have traveled to where you are*. Failure can lurk not only in the shadows of your team, but also in your ability to uphold your character and integrity. That is why, at every step, you need to be cognizant of how you get there. This book has offered you eleven steps on the journey of fulfilling your vision. This last one, however, represents the undertones that must be woven through every decision you make and every action you take.

Something else happened back when Providence Care purchased a run-down Howard Johnson hotel six years into our business. For some, this piece of the story may seem minute or unnoticeable. For me, it was a decision that painted the picture of how every step you take matters. Amid the excitement of transforming the hotel into an independent, assisted-living community and opening another door to the house of *yes*, my operations manager, Mike, and I were doing a walk-through to assess what would be required to renovate and refurbish the 50,000-square-foot space. I don't know what made me look, but I took out the ring of keys we had been handed for the property and opened up the vending machine located on the first floor. The coin box was full! I quickly grabbed a trash can from one of the rooms and began going floor-to-floor to see what every vending machine had to offer. With every turn of the keys, I unearthed a slew of coins. In the end, I was holding a trash can full of nearly $250 in quarters, nickels, and dimes.

Shaking the can in my hands, I thought of my kids and how much they would love to have that loose change. As I made the flippant comment, "I bet my ten-year-old would think of this as all the money in the world!" Mike suggested I pocket the change, but there was no way I could. Taking the change was not the example I wanted to set for Mike or any member of our team. As we stood there, I couldn't help but think back to the lesson my father had taught me long ago, when he was selling manufactured homes. I was sixteen and had decided to go to work with him one sunny August day. After running up the street to grab a quick hot dog for lunch, we swung by the post office on our way back to his office. Years earlier, before his business had grown big enough to have an office, he had rented a P.O. Box. It had not been used for a while, and he figured it was past time to return the box key and close it out. I waited in the car as he walked in to return the key. Coming out, he was holding two crisp $1 bills—the return of his initial deposit. Getting in the car and reaching for his seatbelt, he handed me the money. "Here Johnnie," he said. "Write up a deposit slip for this and make a receipt for it." Make a deposit slip? I thought. Why, for what, it's two dollars! I told my father that was ridiculous and suggested he just put it in his pocket and not waste his time. He refused, and with a stern look he said, "Those dollars are the company's money, not mine." He then said something I never forgot: "Son, you will mess up enough by accident, don't ever do it on purpose." As my father continued to become a dedicated businessman, it was clear to me that was also a man of integrity. His words were imprinted in my mind from that day forward, replaying over and over again as I looked down at the garbage tin full of change.

There was never a moment of indecision. The vending machine money belonged to the company and I was going to put it there, even when that meant paying taxes on it. I turned to Mike, handed him the heavy trash can of coins and told him just as my father had, "Make a deposit slip and deposit this into the corporate account." I could tell he was surprised by my decision, but I remained firm. Mike worked for the company and any and all income to Providence Care was security for him as well. Half of the money also belonged to Dr. Romin, as we were 50/50 business partners. My keeping that money would be like taking it from Mike, Romin, and everyone who was a part of our team. To choose to be unethical with the small things would be me showing my team and customers I could just as easily be unethical with the bigger choices—ones that would have much more impact. I was learning how to build and navigate a new enterprise the best way I knew how: with intention in every step. Leaving the hotel, we drove to the bank and deposited the $250 in the company's general fund.

In moments of decision, where two opposing paths intersect, you will often face a choice between taking the easy route—which may not align with your core values—and leading with integrity. At those pinnacle moments, you have the opportunity to add some of your greatest value and to gain exponential positive influence over those who are watching. That's because even the most seemingly minute actions can have an overwhelming ethical impact and forge a lasting memory. In every step you take—every action or inaction—you are under the microscope. Your legacy is being built every second of every day, in every interaction. It is developing during your easy and exciting times, as well as (perhaps especially) during the most stressful moments. It is shaped by the values you lived by and how you recover when you don't live up to them.

Dr. Wayne Dyer once said that if you want to know who someone is at their core, squeeze them and see what comes out. What comes out during stress and pressure is always founded in either fear or faith, revealing the essence of that person. What will come out of the journey from vision to destination is *who you truly are*! Legacy is not solely about accomplishments—how grand a team you have shaped or how big an enterprise you have built. It is also about how you treated people along the way and the positive impact you have made on your community. It boils down to the experiences you have created in the lives of others. If you haven't figured it out by now, let me tell you plainly. This journey you have been on was *not* ultimately about you starting a business or pursuing your dream; it's about you developing yourself into the best version of yourself, in service to others. It's a spiritual pursuit of greatness and impact. The realization of your dream is just a result of this journey you have chosen to embark on. The time is always *now* to be the kind of person you want others to remember. Because when you reach the goal line, it will have mattered how you got there. This is the final milestone.

Leave a Wake You Are Proud Of

When a boat traverses the water, it will always leave behind it a wake—a ripple or disturbance in what would otherwise be calm waters. When a boat rushes through with excess speed or erratic movement, the wake will mimic that effect. Imagine sitting peacefully in a canoe or on a paddleboard, when a rush of waves come flooding in, unsettling your stance, nearly pushing you overboard. Compare that to a calm wake that you can see coming and find comfort in, knowing it has come from a boat that you have been counting on to guide you through the seas. A wake can be a powerful force and the person at the helm must remain aware of how their decisions and actions are impacting others.

As a leader, you are the person sailing the ship, even if you have handed off the helm and responsibilities to your team. With every twist and turn, you are leaving a wake. Your desired ripple effect should always be to have great people and processes, all moving in the same direction, with positive impact for all stakeholders. That is the foundation for a sustainable legacy. However, it is also built from *how* and *who* you are as the leader shaping all of this. Those coming behind you will remember how you made them feel. This will determine whether they want to follow your lead. It all folds into the adage I mentioned earlier: as the tide comes in, all boats should rise.

Are you raising others up with the trail you leave behind? In order to move forward, you have to look back. When you arrive at your destination, or prepare to embark on the next level of your vision, stop and turn around. This is the one instance where I encourage you to look in the rear-view mirror as you move forward. Check in with your head, but also check in with your heart. Your true feelings will call out any nonsense as you ask yourself:

- *What have you created or destroyed along the way? Are you proud of it?*
- *How many bridges have you burned to get to where you are? How many people have you stepped on? How many people are less because you wanted to become more?* None of these are true success.
- *Are the people you impacted along the way better off for having been on the journey with you?* That is true success!
- *Did you uphold your values the entire time?*
- *Along the way, what opportunities have you had for exponential impact?*
- *If hindsight is 20/20, what would you do differently next time?*

When you are willing to turn around and assess the wake you're leaving behind, you gain a new appreciation for the impact your values, principles, and beliefs can have! Life will always be directed by these elements. They will move you to become someone greater in service to others. They will be what you are known for. A positive impact is only going to happen when your values are true and right. In building your initial or next level vision, as I said, don't ever do anything you'd want to have appear on the front page of the *New York Times* and not be proud of having done. If you aren't seeing the positive impact, it may be time to reassess your actions, decisions, and core values as you expand your vision—or make your exit.

Be Intentionally Present

During one of the many senior staff training sessions at Providence Care, I asked the team who the best multitasker was in the company. Everyone in the room pointed to Kathy, a seasoned nursing director beloved by her team and known for fulfilling many projects. I asked Kathy to show us all how great she was at multitasking. With a sheepish smile she said, "Okay, I'll play along." I then asked her to think about her favorite song.

"Do you have one in mind?" I asked. She answered yep! "Do you know all the words to this song?" She nodded yes. "Great, now think about your second favorite song. Do you know all the words in your mind?" I asked. And Kathy once again nodded yes. "Now sing them both at the same time," I then said. She and the room fell silent.

The fact of the matter is that it doesn't matter how good you are at your role or how talented you think you are, you cannot multitask as well as you think! Our brains are mighty machines, though none of us are able to effectively perform more than one duty at the time. In our modern world, complication has woven its way through countless aspects of our lives and enterprises.

Everything is moving at the speed of our thumbs, grasped tightly around our smartphones. When you are constantly being disrupted by text messages, emails, thoughts, and anxieties, the end result is that you are never fully present where you are! Distraction is everywhere and destroying our ability to be fully present in the moment. Right here, right now is the only time any of us are really ever promised.

Being intentionally present is about accepting the challenge to focus well on one task at a time and to be truly in the present moment. Carpe diem? Not exactly. After working in hospice care for fifteen years, I believe that *carpe momentum* (seize the moments) is a more accurate intent. Life is not a series of days, months, or years; it's a string of moments. The small things don't just mean a lot, they mean everything. The small moments are the impact points that shape how you get to where you are, and it's up to you to make *every single moment count.*

Shaping a big vision into a reality is an enormous feat. There's no denying that the demands and doldrums along the way can feel like they require all of your attention and energy. However, it's critical to maintain awareness that multitasking often leads to missed moments! Delete or barely glance at a small, seemingly meaningless thing could end up meaning everything. Taking on too many tasks at once can mean you are not fully giving of yourself to any of them. Be mindful of the tendencies to become distracted or to attempt taking on too much at once. Take hold of these moments and flip them around to become more present. Always make every interaction and decision matter, because the meaning you give to small moments will affect your ability to effectively navigate them and leave a wake you can be proud of. Here are some questions to consider to help keep you centered in the moment as you progress along your leadership journey:

- *How can you commit yourself to being the best version of yourself in every moment?*
- *What situations test your ability to stay on a path of presence, intention, and integrity?*
- *Going forward, can you combine tasks only when they complement each other?* For instance, you are listening to a podcast (feeding your mind) while running on a treadmill (exercising your body.)
- *Can you be careful not to discount or delete anything you initially feel doesn't speak to where you are at the present moment? Could it serve to open you up to learning something new?*

We typically don't remember a day, a month, or a year; we remember small moments of meaning. I don't recall what I wore on the day that my wife went into labor with our third daughter. I don't recall opening the door to the hospital when we walked in for the delivery, yet I know we did. I don't even remember much of the chaos of the scene during the labor. I do remember however the moment Kelley looked at me with apprehensive excitement and said, "This baby is coming *now* and I guess it's just going to be you and me here, huh?" I'll never forget the moments of holding my new baby girl for the first time. I bet you have moments right now that speak to you just the same. Do your best to capture every opportunity you are given to be present, making each matter by slowing down enough to not just look at those who are with you, but to truly see and understand them. Amplify your presence in every moment, and your life, relationships, and impact will change for the better. That is what it takes to be a leader worth following.

Protect Your Relationships

Two years into starting Providence Care, I was in the throes of turmoil. It was mainly with myself, my own insecurities, and the unknowns of business. It felt like I was walking through the wilderness as a tangled ball of stress, trying to manage the overwhelming day-to-day as best as I could. Even with years of industry experience and learning, I continued to see my share of failures, gains, and moments that stretched me and what I thought was possible. Building Providence Care required so much of me, but despite my passion, there was a downside. I was neglecting my wife and family. Even when I was physically available to them, I was a million miles away emotionally, swimming in my sea of worry about the agency.

Months would pass, and Kelley would remind me of what was most important: family, balance, and our faith. I would tell her she had the luxury of worrying about such things because I was carrying the weight of a new business, our employees, our patients, and their families on my shoulders. I once felt justified enough in my state of self-righteousness that I told her that she didn't understand the stress I was under, questioning whether I could truly fulfill my vision. Enemies and competition seemed to be lurking everywhere and there were countless mistakes just waiting to be made. I felt engulfed in it all. I did my best to explain that what I was trying to navigate was like playing 3D chess on the bow of a sailboat, in the middle of a hurricane. There was so much pressure to not let one chess piece fall, while at the same time as so many forces were working against me. I had to watch every move and counter move, all the while having a plan for every contingency. It also didn't help that I was playing against some of the most successful, talented, and experienced players in the industry. One wrong move could destroy everything.

As I finished my rant, Kelley got up and began to walk away. Then she stopped suddenly. Turning toward me, she looked me in the eyes and said, "You can continue to focus on all those things that may or may not happen, but remember one thing: the only way you will ever win at this game is to ensure that every move you make protects your queen." She then turned and walked out of the room. Well played and point made. She was right. Kelley and Romin had lived this journey with me every day and I needed to protect them, along with the rest of my family. Kelley had granted me a healthy dose of perspective. It helped me find my way back to the true meaning and importance of what I was building.

True success means finding the balance where your personal and professional lives meet. Energy flows to where your attention goes. When you haven't been paying attention to your family, health, spirituality, hobbies, friendships and financial affairs, you have neglected that part of you, and you will never be truly fulfilled. Success cannot be a solo journey. Your ultimate wealth will always lie within your health and the bonds you have with those you love. Fulfilling your vision without fulfilling personal relationships is worthless. This journey of shaping your vision into a team was never all about you. Love and prioritize the people who are going to be with you after your journey of shaping your vision is over. Continuously check in with yourself and ask whether you are protecting your queens (or kings). When the balance between caring for your health and family is off, refocus on the areas that you neglected—intentionally or not. Only then will you be able to serve everyone at the level you intended.

You are in pursuit of changing lives of those around you on a grand level. That's why you are in business, but you can't do it to the detriment of the people you love. Take care of your relationships, and make sure that you are proud of whatever you do. That's because what you are not focused on, you are going to neglect. Remember, whatever you mismanage is ultimately taken from you. Money in the bank account is just a means to get to where you want to be in life, but none of that means anything if you are the wealthiest person, living in your mansion alone, or the richest person in the graveyard. True joy comes from sharing those moments with those you love and who love you.

The Key Questions

It Matters How You Get There

- Leave a Wake You Are Proud Of:
    - *What would you do differently knowing what you know now?*
    - *How can you change to align with this clarity?*
- Be Intentionally Present:
    - *What techniques can you use to focus, slow down, and minimize distractions?*

  - *What can you do or change to ensure you seize the key moments every day?*

- Protect Your Relationships:
  - *Why are you doing what you're doing? Who are you doing it for?*
  - *What can you change today to protect the relationships you have with those you love the most?*

Take Action

1. **Look around and gauge your speed:** Your wake is a lagging indicator of what you have already done. The best thing you can do to ensure you leave a wake you are proud of is to prepare before you enter a situation or decision path. Look around and assess the next hundred yards. Have the foresight to know what your surroundings are going to be, and who will be impacted. Look closely at yourself and monitor and mirror the others involved. The speed at which you try to achieve any goal also matters greatly. Before you begin at any speed, ask yourself what is required, who is involved, and what is acceptable to them.
2. **Decrease your distractions:** Look at your calendar every day and break things down. How intentional are you being with your time? How much are you prioritizing the various areas of your life and business/team? Evaluate this balance daily and cut back on

distractions delaying you from focusing on what truly matters—at work and at home. Prioritization increases yield, because it allows you to be present in each moment, doing as you intended to do. The quality of your life will be a direct result of the quality of your habits. Be intentional.

3. **Assess the impact on your relationships:** Go to the people closest to you and those affected by your daily decisions within your team. Ask them if you are showing up as you need to—as a spouse, a leader, a friend, a parent, or a colleague. When their responses lead to realize you are not being all you want to be to those who matter most, then stop and reassess. How can you become more present with them in order to nourish those relationships?

When you look at your current reality, versus when you initiated your vision, how have you changed? How has your enterprise evolved? How is the vision now different than you thought it would be? Excellence is not for the faint of heart! You are already a different person from when you began; you are going to be a different person the more you evolve. Challenge yourself and what you have built to continue to grow up and mature, and you will experience a continuous rebirth and renewal. With every step you take, do so by being conscious of the wake you are leaving, being present in the moment, and nurturing the relationships that matter the most. These are the elements that fuel true sustainability, success, and significance. These are the elements that disrupt failure at the highest level. You can build a great team and culture, master sales, and structure smart systems, but it won't hold the same weight without your integrity and presence. Become an active force for good and for growth. Life is constantly evolving and you must grow with it. The principles in this chapter will further strengthen the foundation you have built, so it can withstand every storm and the test of time. It matters how you get to where you are going—whether that means continuing to grow what you started or making an exit. However, *it's how you end that matters most.* Do what needs to be done to rebalance and refocus. End on an upswing. Only then will you have mastered disrupting failure.

THE MILESTONE MAP

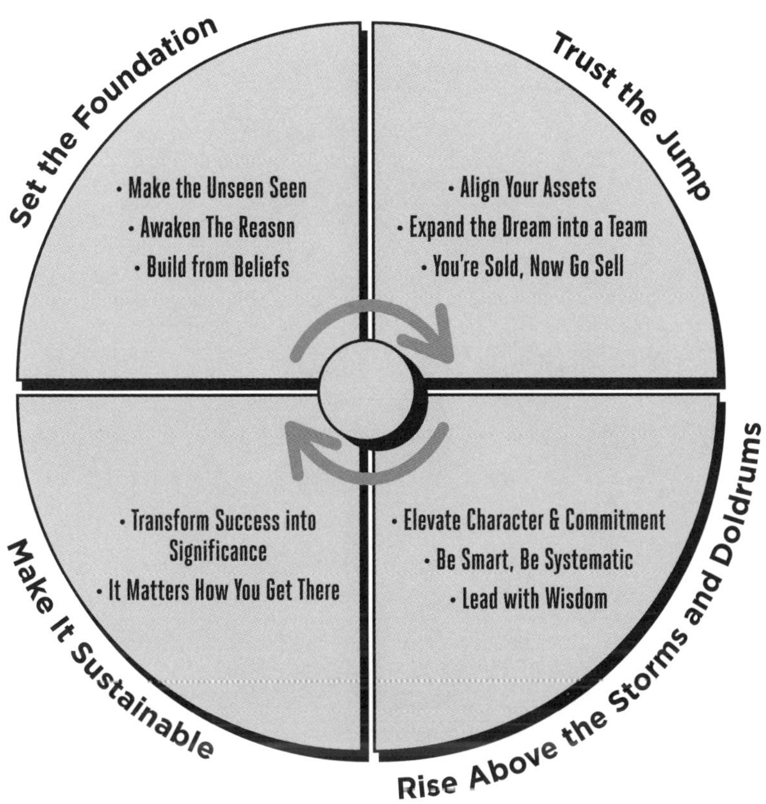

SET THE FOUNDATION

Milestone 1: Make the Unseen Seen

Imagine a better tomorrow and form a vision of what right looks like to you. Identify opportunities and solutions where others see problems or blindly accept the status quo.

Milestone 2: Awaken the Reason

You had better know your *why*! Get clear on what is motivating you, what you can lean on when things get hard, and whether the realization of your vision is worth the price you will pay.

Milestone 3: Build from Beliefs

Culture is birthed from norms, rules, and spoken and unspoken traditions. If you don't choose your culture, it will choose you! Create the core beliefs that will guide how people treat each other and processes intended to be followed.

TRUST THE JUMP

Milestone 4: Align Your Assets

At least eighty percent of your success stems from taking consistent action—the twenty percent. You will be the fuel behind your vision, team, and sales—the elements that will carry you through to success.

Milestone 5: Expand the Dream to a Team

Begin to create an ideal team that has cohesion and camaraderie. Do so through an environment where clarity of vision rules, there exists a complete sense of belonging, and there is trust among team members.

Milestone 6: You're Sold, Now Go Sell!

Establish a process for finding your target customer and helping your team confidently exchange your vision for sales. Ensure constant advocacy by making everyone an ambassador for your product or service.

RISE ABOVE THE STORMS AND DOLDRUMS

Milestone 7: Elevate Character and Commitment

As you encounter storms and doldrums, things grow tougher in a very real and raw way. You may begin considering potential exit ramps. Choose to see challenges as opportunities to build character and commitment and you will rise to every occasion, no matter how hard.

Milestone 8: Be Smart, Be Systematic

It's time to make everything run like clockwork. Shape a reproducible process for solving problems—one that your team can run to deliver a high-quality, predictable experience, over and over again.

Milestone 9: Lead with Wisdom

Allow your impact catch fire and fuel sustainability by optimizing the systems, processes, and information sharing that sustain success. Do so as you take innovative action to capture new opportunities.

MAKE IT SUSTAINABLE

Milestone 10: Transform Success into Significance

Allow money, wisdom, and knowledge to flow *through* you and not *to* you. Release what you no longer need to hold on to, making room for new opportunities, growth, and the ability to make those around you even better leaders.

Milestone 11: It Matters How You Get There

Your legacy is being built every second of every day, in every interaction—during the easy and exciting times as well as the most strenuous moments and deep in the biggest doldrums. Live by the values you established early on, and know how to recover when you don't live up to them.

JOHNNIE'S TERMS

Character: the capacity to endure pain and use wisdom to find joy

Commitment: to continue when you don't feel like it

Consistency: the ability to recreate a desired result at will

Core Values (Beliefs): the personal standards that dictate your behavior

Culture: the way we do things around here

Decision: when a desired outcome never has occurred but yet you continue to try

Doldrum: a challenge or problem to be overcome

Doors to the House of *Yes*: innovating by expanding your product or service offering

Failure: a lagging indicator of what you have *not* done in the past six to twelve months

Foundation: the base that holds up everything else

HR: Human Relationships

In Season: the right time is to do the right thing

Innovation: expanding your identity

Legacy: how people talk about you behind your back

Luck: where preparation meets opportunity

Motivation: what is guiding you, the reason behind your work

Opportunity: a chance to open more doors to the house of *yes*

Passion: what must always precede profits

Problem: when a desired outcome used to occur and now it no longer does

Processes: how you will effectively execute and manage your systems

Profit: the monetary echo of your ability to create value for others

Progress: taking the actions you know you can in every moment

Relationships: happen when you make a genuine attempt to learn about others' needs, wants, goals, and desires

Sales: the exchange of one mode of value for another and the process whereby an individual pursues their wants, needs, or desires through the cooperation of someone else

Standards: the conditions of life you are willing (or no longer willing) to accept for yourself and those you love

Success: a lagging indicator and byproduct of what you have done in the past six to twelve months

Sustainability: prolonged success brought forth through consistency and discipline

Talent: behaviors and abilities that come naturally and for which people don't need to work very hard to achieve

Team: those who have committed to support one another with a shared vision through common beliefs

Trust: the consistent fulfillment of expectations

Vision: an intention, a purpose statement, an outcome, a goal, an objective of what could be

What Right Looks Like: the idealized best version of a result

Wisdom: the ability to know the facts while recognizing the truth

ENDNOTES

1 "Everest 1953: First Footsteps—Sir Edmund Hillary and Tenzing Norgay," *National Geographic*, March 3, 2013, https://www.nationalgeographic.com/adventure/article/sir-edmund-hillary-tenzing-norgay-1953.

2 "The Lottery Curse: Are Lottery Winners More Likely to Declare Bankruptcy?" American Bankruptcy Institute, https://www.abi.org/feed-item/the-lottery-curse-are-lottery-winners-more-likely-to-declare-bankruptcy.